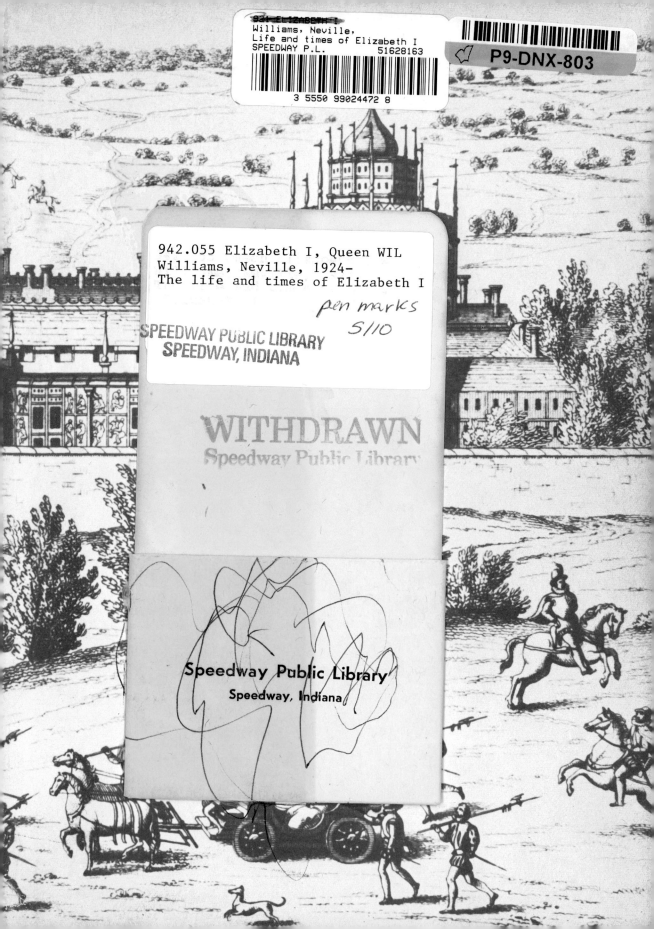

The Life and Times of
ELIZABETH I

The Life and Times of
ELIZABETH I

Neville Williams

Introduction by Antonia Fraser

Doubleday & Company
Garden City, New York
1972

For my niece, Elizabeth Churchill

Designed by Rodney Josey
Filmset by Keyspools Limited, Golborne, Lancashire
Printed in Great Britain by
C. Tinling & Co. Ltd, London and Prescot

Contents

A*

Introduction

Y OU MAY WELL HAVE a greater prince, but you shall never have a more loving prince': these famous words of Queen Elizabeth I, spoken to her loyal subjects in December 1588 following the defeat of the Spanish Armada, still ring in our ears. There are many indeed who feel that we shall never have 'a greater prince', let alone a more loving one, than Elizabeth Tudor, daughter of Henry VIII and Anne Boleyn – but this is a matter for personal preference. It is however the impression which Elizabeth conveyed, that above all she loved her English people, which makes her unique among our sovereigns. This concept of a queen wedded to her subjects was brilliantly expressed in her life style: it seemed that neither Leicester for love nor the French prince Alençon for political advantage could ever quite supplant the English people in her heart. There was to be no other bridegroom during her long reign.

How was this satisfying picture put across so effectively in 'an age of Queens', when Elizabeth's sister rulers were compelled to marry – and marry disastrously? Was it quite simply the truth about Elizabeth that, whatever her dalliance with favourites such as Hatton and Essex, ultimately her affections were bestowed on the people she ruled, or was she on the contrary the supreme calculating exponent of the public image, who turned an apparent disadvantage – her feminity – into cool advantage? Certainly the cruel reverses of her childhood were enough to teach Elizabeth that she had to be cunning in order to survive, with her mother executed as an adulteress, herself declared a bastard from having been hailed as heiress to the throne, and her half-sister Queen Mary Tudor completing the cycle by imprisoning her for conspiracy. It was hardly surprising that one courtier remarked of her in youth that 'she has a very good wit, and nothing is gotten of her but by great policy'. As for her femininity, the whole question of which gains further poignancy today when the role of women is so much discussed, Queen Elizabeth herself declared publicly that she was the equal of any man: 'And though I be a woman, yet I have as good courage, answerable to my place, as ever my father had.' But perhaps Robert Cecil spoke more of the truth in his perceptive observation that she might be 'more than a man' but she was also 'sometimes (by troth) less than a woman'.

7

It is such unresolved questions as these about the mysterious inner character of Gloriana, the outwardly glittering centre of a splendid court, which make her such an eternally fascinating subject for biography. Above all, the Queen herself never lost sight of the fact that she was the ruler of her country – 'Elizabeth R'. The conflicts between the two roles of Queen and woman, are here lucidly analysed by Neville Williams. This was an intensely political age, and also an age of fierce religious controversy. Elizabeth threaded her way through such mazes of difficulty to become, as Neville Williams puts it 'the first monarch to give her name to an age'. Our feeling of certainty that the reign was a success, that the Elizabeth age was glorious in our history as a moment when we arrived at true national consciousness, contrasts with our uncertainties about the personality of Elizabeth herself. It is the effect of this contrast that we continue to be enthralled by the life and times of Queen Elizabeth I, just as four centuries earlier Elizabeth, 'their loving prince', enthralled our ancestors.

Antonia Fraser

Author's preface

THIS SHORT BIOGRAPHY of England's most remarkable Queen emphasises the chief aspects of her life which, in my opinion, are most important for an understanding of her character and the significance of her long reign, during which the people of England attained a true national consciousness. A book of this kind is necessarily grounded on the work of many specialists in Tudor studies and it would be invidious to single out particular names. Throughout its preparation, however, I have been guided and encouraged by Christopher Falkus and in the later stages have been grateful for the generous advice of Margaret Willes with regard to both text and illustration. I also wish to thank Diana Steer for her speedy and efficient typing of my manuscript.

N.W.

1 The Path
to the Throne 1533-58

IN THE RIVERSIDE PALACE of Greenwich, in September 1533, the Queen's apartments were prepared for Anne Boleyn's lying-in. A splendid bed, that had once formed part of the ransom of a French prince, had been brought out of the Treasury at Westminster and sent by barge to Henry VIII's favourite residence and his own birthplace, where he now anxiously awaited that child of the English Reformation, the prince for whom he had waited so long. None of Catherine of Aragon's sons had lived and, after years of frustration, Henry had convinced himself that their marriage had been unlawful in the sight of God because she had, if only briefly, been the wife of his sickly brother. For six years Henry had vainly tried to obtain

Henry VIII, a detail from
a full-length portrait by
Holbein, painted in about
1536.

12

a divorce from the Pope to enable him to marry the Lady Anne, the younger daughter of Sir Thomas Boleyn, Earl of Wiltshire, who had completely captivated him, and when negotiations finally failed he had taken the momentous step of breaking from the Church of Rome.

Anne's great-grandfather, a mercer, had been Lord Mayor of London in 1457, but her grandfather had abandoned trade to develop his estates in Norfolk and had married the Earl of Ormonde's daughter. Her father, a younger son, succeeded in marrying a Howard, who bore him three children, Mary, probably born in 1503, George in 1505, and Anne two years later at their Kentish home, Hever Castle. Sir Thomas had been

LEFT Anne Boleyn, Elizabeth's mother and Henry VIII's second wife. Portrait by an unknown artist.

OVERLEAF, RIGHT Hampton Court, the great house inherited by Henry VIII from Cardinal Wolsey, which he turned into a magnificent palace.

OVERLEAF, LEFT Princess Elizabeth at about the age of twelve. Her love of books and learning is already evident in this portrait by an unknown artist.

created a Knight of the Bath at Henry's coronation and was soon employed on diplomatic missions which enabled both his daughters to be brought up in the sophisticated court of Queen Claude of France. By 1520, Mary Boleyn had married William Carey of the Privy Chamber, but almost at once became the King's mistress. Anne stayed in France until 1522, and when she made her début at the English court she was reckoned so graceful that no one would have known she was English. Mary's liaison with the King had earned Sir Thomas's elevation to the peerage in 1525 and his appointment as Lord Privy Seal, though by this time Henry was tiring of her. Early in 1526 he fell passionately in love with Anne, with her beautiful black, almond-shaped eyes. She had refused the undignified role of mistress that had satisfied her elder sister, for she had set her heart on becoming Queen. Indeed, even before they had met, Henry was talking of putting away Catherine of Aragon, for he despaired of her producing a son for him. Henry had waited for nearly seven years to see the successful conclusion of his 'great matter', fraught with immense consequences for England and its people, and now he awaited the coming acquisition of a male heir.

Henry and Anne had probably been living as man and wife since their state visit to France in the autumn of 1532, but it was not until January that they were married in secret, when she was already with child. In May Archbishop Cranmer pronounced the King's marriage to Catherine void and proclaimed Anne to be his lawful wife; she was crowned Queen on Whitsun Day and looked forward to overturning her detractors by triumphantly providing England with a male heir. On Sunday, 7 September she was delivered of her baby, who confounded her parents by being a girl. Their disappointment was acute: the prayers of the Church had been totally ineffectual, it seemed,

16

ABOVE Greenwich Palace, where Elizabeth was born in September 1533. This drawing was made by Anthony van Wyngaerde, Flemish visitor to England in the 1550s.

as had the prognostications of the astrologers who had all predicted a son. It was not for a female child that Henry had defied the Pope, and he could not bring himself to attend her christening three days later when she was named Elizabeth after his mother, Elizabeth of York, who had herself been the daughter of another Elizabeth, the queen of Edward IV.

As she grew up the Princess was to lay great store on being 'mere English', and this was the key to her popularity. She had not a trace of foreign blood in her veins in marked contrast to her sister Mary, who was half Spanish, and she was never to set foot outside her native land, not even to visit the Wales of her grandfather, Henry Tudor. Her enemies saw her as the symbol of England's breach with Catholic Europe and the threat to Mary's birthright. To her father the perils of a woman's rule seemed insufferable, yet Elizabeth was destined to become one of the most remarkable queens of all time. For the present, there seemed little likelihood of Elizabeth succeeding to the throne, for her father took comfort in the fact that she was a healthy baby, and that before long a healthy son would follow. Moreover, his natural son by Elizabeth Blount had been groomed for the succession ever since his creation as Duke of Richmond in 1525. It was not until his death in the summer of 1536 that Elizabeth was generally regarded as heir-presumptive.

BELOW The old Palace at Hatfield, originally built by Henry VII's Cardinal Morton, but used by Henry as a childhood home for both Elizabeth and Mary. It was while staying here in 1558 that Elizabeth received the news of Mary's death and her own accession to the throne.

Since court was no place for an infant, Elizabeth was soon taken from her mother, as was customary, and placed under the care of Lady Bryan at Hatfield Palace in Hertfordshire. She was to spend most of her first ten years at Hatfield, or at neighbouring houses at Hunsdon and Ashridge near Berkhamsted, and the manor of the More that had belonged to Cardinal Wolsey, all of them in good country air away from the plague and smoke of London. Mary, the child of Catherine of Aragon, now nearly eighteen and deprived of her title of Princess of Wales, was ordered by King Henry to become a maid-of-honour to her baby half-sister, and when she proved obstinate Anne Boleyn demanded that her ears be boxed for being a 'cursed bastard'. Henry was proud of his little daughter and had her brought to court for special occasions, while Mary was kept away. Elizabeth, in her turn, marvelled at the enormous, imperious figure who was her father, and while he lived he was her idol, supreme in Church and State, the one man who could do no wrong. At the beginning of 1536, when the King celebrated the death of Catherine of Aragon clad entirely in yellow, he carried Elizabeth in his arms after dinner, showing her off to courtiers. Later that month, Anne Boleyn miscarried of a male child and experiencing Henry's fury, knew that she would not be given another chance. Henry determined to put her away, convinced that her baby was deformed and that when he had married her he had been 'seduced by witchcraft'. It was not difficult for Cromwell's spies to bring together evidence suggesting that Anne had enjoyed sexual relations with five men, including her brother. In May Elizabeth was at Greenwich when her mother was arrested and sent on her way to trial and execution for adultery. The child had seen her mother so rarely that her death meant little to her at this time.

Elizabeth, like Mary, became branded as illegitimate following her father's marriage to Jane Seymour, and the Princess's household at Hunsdon was forced to be run on a reduced budget. Lady Bryan, who was devoted to her young charge, complained to Thomas Cromwell about her lack of essential clothes, as well as about the foolish attitude of pompous Sir John Shelton, the steward of the house, who had ordered that the child should take her meals in the hall with her elders, when what she needed was simple nursery fare in her own room,

18

especially as she was teething. Elizabeth's first public duties were at Prince Edward's christening, just after her fourth birthday, when she bore the baptismal robe in procession at Hampton Court, being carried herself by the Prince's uncle, Edward Seymour, who was to rule England as Protector after King Henry's death. The baby Prince joined his sisters' household in the country and at once became the centre of Lady Bryan's world. Elizabeth accepted without question that she must give way to her brother, who was undisputed heir to the throne, and she became very fond of him, for example sewing him a cambric shirt. The fact that Jane Seymour had died in childbed made for a further bond between brother and sister.

Kate Champernowne, a Devonshire blue-stocking, who was highly regarded by Roger Ascham and the Cambridge humanists, became Elizabeth's governess, laying the foundations of an extensive classical education in the Renaissance tradition. For relaxation there was dancing, riding, archery, and needlework which the Princess hated, and above all music, which she loved. Princess Mary taught her various card games, which they would play for small stakes, and she enjoyed the repartee of Jane the Fool and the antics of Lucretia, a tumbler. Her father was sent frequent reports of her progress, but she saw him only rarely, and it was fortunate that she escaped the corrupting influence of the court during his marriage to her aunt, Catherine Howard, who in 1540 supplanted the incompatible but kindly Anne of Cleves. Catherine's execution for adultery in 1542 closely followed the fate of Anne Boleyn, except that Catherine Howard left no infant behind her. We shall never know how these episodes in King Henry's matrimonial ventures were related to Elizabeth, but their effect on her was profound. One thing is certain: he had become a grotesque Goliath, sickly and full of self pity, but he was always her hero, and though they were not often together, Henry remained the one constant factor in her childhood. He embodied the new monarchy of the Reformation, supreme in Church and State, ruling in the image of God, and Elizabeth was fascinated by his power and wealth. The man who could dethrone the Pope, dissolve the monasteries, change his wife or chief minister at a whim, compose songs and build Nonsuch Palace was no ordinary father; she worshipped him and was always to revere his

KATHARINE PARRE

Catherine Parr, Henry VIII's sixth and last Queen. Catherine took great interest in Elizabeth, encouraging her love of learning. After Henry's death in 1547, Catherine married the unprincipled Lord Thomas Seymour, and took Elizabeth to live with them at Chelsea and Hanworth.

achievement. Having such a father made up for having no mother and made her illegitimate status of comparatively little significance.

At last in 1543, with Henry's marriage to his sixth wife, Catherine Parr, the royal children were brought to court for much of the year and Elizabeth, now ten, could feel she had a more settled home as well as a step-mother who took a real interest in her. Catherine, one of the most cultivated women of her generation, encouraged the girl's bookishness and her flair for languages and persuaded Henry to extend her formal education. She was allowed to share Prince Edward's tutors, so that Sir John Cheke taught her Greek and Roger Ascham Latin. She was launched on Italian and taught to write a beautiful Italic script. Queen Catherine herself directed her study of divinity, helping her to master the Early Fathers as well as the Greek New Testament. She was delighted with the Princess's New Year's gift for her – a translation in Latin, French and

20

Italian of the Queen's own prayers and meditations. Romances were banned, but stories from classical mythology, history and the Bible could be read, provided they pointed a moral. It seemed as if Erasmus's hopes that the English court would become a university had been fulfilled. In the Reformation era theological controversy remained high politics, so that all this godly learning had great practical relevance, yet Elizabeth loved learning for its own sake and retained to her death the scholar's habit of translating and annotating. Moreover, her fluency in Latin, French and Italian enabled her as Queen to speak to foreign envoys and read letters from abroad without the need for interpreters.

A portrait of these years shows a pale-faced girl with auburn hair and innocent eyes, wearing a simple gown of crimson cloth of gold and few jewels: regal, indeed, in her bearing, but still a child. Elizabeth is depicted as the industrious student, absorbed in her books. The last three years of Henry VIII's reign were the most placid of her whole life; but by 1547, he was dead. Despite the careful arrangements in Henry's will for a council of regency, Edward Seymour, Earl of Hertford – who was uncle to Edward VI – seized power to become Protector during Edward's minority and embarked on a policy which turned England into a Protestant state. King Henry had held complete trust in Seymour during the final months of his life and had earlier appointed him lieutenant of the kingdom in his absence during the last French war. Seymour himself had won the laurels of war and engineered the fall of the Howards, his bitterest opponents, as Henry lay dying. Now, with his nephew safely on the throne, he was supreme. For the present Elizabeth stayed with Catherine Parr in her dower house at Chelsea, but the future was fraught with problems.

The Protector, now Duke of Somerset, created his brother Lord Thomas Seymour and appointed him Lord High Admiral, but denied him real power. Thomas plotted to oust his brother, and as a first step, having considered the possibilities of winning one of the Princesses, married the Queen Dowager, whom he had courted before King Henry had shown any interest in her. Installed at Chelsea, this unprincipled rake began to flirt with Elizabeth in a teasing way, stealing kisses from her, brazenly smacking her, giving her hugs and tickles that made her blush.

Elizabeth's New Year's gift to Catherine Parr in 1545, a translation of the Queen's prayers and meditations into Latin, French and Italian. The dedication page is shown here.

RATIONI, O VERO ME
...tationi dalle quali la mente
...ncitata a patientemente pa
...c ogni afflittione, et fprezzare
...vana profperita di quefto mõ
..., et fempre defiderare l'eterna
...atitudine:raccolte da alcune
...ate opere, per la valorofsima,
...umanifsima princefsa, Cathe
...a reina d'inghilterra, francia
...hibernia. Tradotte per la figno
...Elizabetta dalla lingua inglefe
...vulgare italiano.

Lord Thomas Seymour of Sudeley, Lord High Admiral, by an unknown artist. His schemes during Edward VI's reign to marry the Princess Elizabeth ultimately cost him his head, and almost brought Elizabeth to the block.

One day in the garden, while Catherine held her, he slashed the black dress she was wearing into a hundred pieces with his sword; and then of a morning, while still in his nightgown, he would come into her bedroom, draw back the curtains of the four-poster bed and pretend he was going to leap onto her, while she hid herself under the bedclothes. Her old governess, Kate Champernowne, who had married John Ashley but remained in the Princess's service, told the Admiral he was ruining the girl's reputation. Elizabeth had the sense to be fully dressed well before Seymour next broke into her room, and did not look up from her book. Clearly, she had been attracted to

22

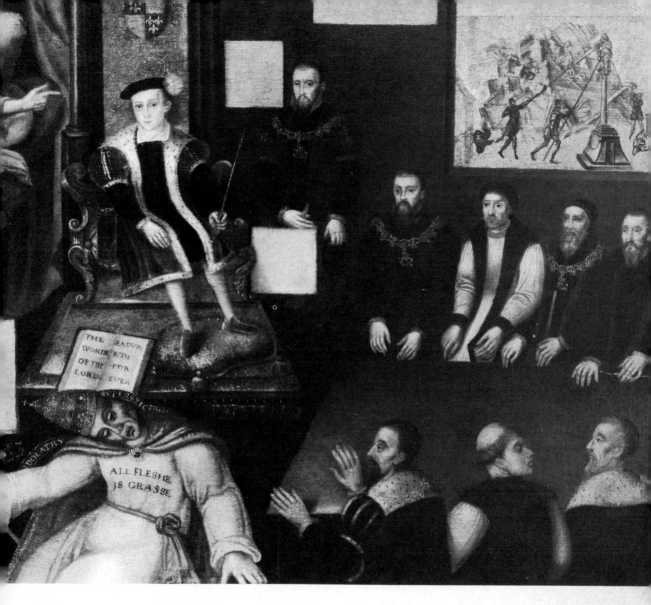

The text in the image includes:

THE READUR WORDE ETH OF THE FOR LORDS EVER

ALL FLESHE IS GRASSE

this handsome man and was flattered that he bothered to give her so much of his attention. At fourteen one kiss would have startled her sexual emotions, but his motives were too transparent. Her modesty was shocked by his mock attempts at seduction and the rather risky escapades degenerated into a bedroom farce which she could laugh at until the repetition of the same old jokes and gestures became too pathetic. For all his charm the Admiral had become repulsive and she was determined that he would never come across her alone.

During her pregnancy Catherine Parr's jealousy of the Princess increased, and at Whitsun 1548 she caught Elizabeth in

An anti-papal allegory of the death-bed of Henry VIII, painted in about 1548. Henry VIII is on the left gesturing to his successor. Edward VI. To Edward's left are the Lord Protector and the Council, Northumberland, Cranmer, and Bedford. This painting probably commemorates Cranmer's order for the destruction of religious images.

23

Seymour's arms. This was too much for Catherine to bear and she insisted on Elizabeth leaving next day for Cheshunt, where she was looked after by Sir Anthony Denny, Kate Ashley's brother-in-law. From Cheshunt she wrote to Queen Catherine tactfully thanking her for her many kindnesses over the years and hoping that she retained a good opinion of her. In retrospect it was clear to Elizabeth that she and Seymour had been playing with fire; it was merciful that she was no more than scorched and, despite his forthright advances, she remained a virgin.

Mistress Ashley had accompanied her to Cheshunt, and it was due to her that Roger Ascham now played a greater part in Elizabeth's education. Ascham regarded her grasp of Latin as exceptional, her Greek commendable and her fluency in French and Italian a noble example. He favoured the system of double translation, turning a portion of Latin prose into English and back again into Latin, and he always regarded her as his brightest pupil. The girl's perseverance in any task was equal to a man's; her memory was prodigious and her musicianship no less professional than her father's. 'In adornment she is elegant, rather than showy', disliking an elaborate hair-style and gold ornaments. '... I teach her words and she [teaches] me things. I teach her the tongues to speak, and her modest and maidenly looks teach me works to do.' Here was the answer, indeed, to any who accused her of being a shameless young hussy in the romps with the Admiral.

Seymour had by no means forgotten her and when Catherine Parr died in childbed at Sudeley he hoped to marry the Princess. Kate Ashley told her bluntly: 'Now he is free again, you may have him if you will.' 'Nay' she replied, blushing. But Mistress Ashley hoped that she would not continue to decline his advances if Protector Somerset and his Council pressed her. When a rumour was related at Cheshunt that she and the Admiral were to be married, the girl brushed it aside; 'It was but a London news', she said, yet those about her were convinced she was most kindly disposed to Seymour. The Admiral now planned to kidnap the young King and marry him to his ward, Lady Jane Grey, chief claimant to the throne from the Suffolk line, for Henry VIII's younger sister, Mary, was her grandmother. But these and other schemes were too blatant for his brother the Protector, and in January 1549 Thomas was sent to the Tower.

24

Roger Ascham, Elizabeth's tutor. He found Elizabeth exceptional at languages, both ancient and modern, and always regarded her as his brightest pupil.

To assemble further incriminating evidence against him, Kate Ashley and Thomas Parry, the cofferer of the Princess's household, were arrested and questioned in the Tower, while a grave Councillor, Sir Robert Tyrwhit, was sent to Elizabeth, now at Hatfield, to glean what he could. Amidst tears the girl remained circumspect; 'she hath a very good wit and nothing is gotten of her but by great policy', wrote Tyrwhit, and she agreed to write to Protector Somerset, denying that Mistress Ashley had ever advised her to marry the Admiral, saying that she would never dream of contracting a match unless the Council gave their consent, and then with great spirit she asked for an official denial of the foul rumours that she was carrying a child of Seymour's; let her come to court and convince people of her innocence.

To try to break her spirit, she was shown the confessions of Kate Ashley and Parry which set down the episodes with Seymour at Chelsea and alluded to the whisperings in the household. She commented that it was a great matter for Master Parry to swear never to confess confidential talk and then to break his promise, but what perturbed her most was the rough treatment of Kate Ashley, confined in a dark cell, cold and hungry. Such treatment of her trusted servant hurt her to the quick and she was furious. When Lady Tyrwhit told her she had come to take Mistress Ashley's place Elizabeth wept and said she would never countenance it. A further tactful letter to Somerset that related a few additional points about Seymour, harmless enough in themselves, convinced the Protector of the girl's innocence. Her servants were released from the Tower and in the summer were permitted to return to her household at Hatfield, but Seymour went to the block. In the catalogue of his high treason was the charge of attempting by crafty means to marry the Princess. She provided a fitting epitaph for him – 'a man of much wit and little judgment'. The association of her name with Seymour's, however, left her in disgrace and her young brother would not receive her at court. More important, the strain of the past eighteen months had affected her health, and she was laid low by nervous exhaustion. The significance of the Seymour episode was this: at the age of fifteen Elizabeth lost to the executioner a man who had succeeded in arousing her love; it seemed to her that she had begun to tread the strange steps of the courtly dance of love and death, romance and tragedy in which her own mother had stumbled and fallen. She would not easily forget the Admiral or the political dangers in which his foolishness had placed her, and for the present she steered clear from politics and from friendships with the opposite sex; a Princess was too vulnerable to play such a game.

In the second half of Edward's reign, when power was concentrated in the hands of John Dudley, Duke of Northumberland, who had succeeded in bringing about Somerset's downfall, and planned to put into effect a more radical political and religious programme, Elizabeth remained quietly in Hertfordshire working hard at her studies and conserving her strength. Life was mercifully uneventful, though she missed her royal brother's company and would send him cheery letters in Latin, full of learned allusions, much as a girl today might send postcards to an absent younger brother. When an artist had finished her portrait at Ashridge, she sent it to Edward with a characteristic note: 'For the face, I grant I may well blush to offer, but the mind I shall never be ashamed to present', and she wished it were herself and not the canvas copy that was sharing his company. News of Edward's last illness was kept from her. Northumberland was confident of his plans for a Protestant succession that would keep him in power, for he had married his son Guildford Dudley to Lady Jane Grey, Henry's great-niece. When Northumberland ordered Elizabeth to the King's bedside, she knew she would be putting her head in a noose. She was, she said, too ill to travel and followed her excuse with a medical certificate. From Hatfield she waited on events and once Northumberland's *coup* had failed, and both country and capital rallied to Mary, she wrote to her sister to congratulate her on her succession and asked for guidance as to when she should come to court to pay her own sisterly homage.

Elizabeth's experiences in her brother's reign had taught her the importance of being on her guard, and in the next five years she was to need all her dissimulation, procrastination and inborn cunning to save herself from Mary's wrath and from the wiles of her well-wishers who were to weave plots around her. Her popularity grew with Mary's plans to marry Philip of Spain and to return England to papal obedience, but Elizabeth was careful to disown it. Age and personality were both on her side and could become fearsome liabilities. The Princess's 'figure and face are very handsome', wrote an ambassador, 'and such an air of dignified majesty pervades all her actions that no one can fail to suppose she is a Queen'. That was the trouble, for therein lay danger. The heir to a throne was in an invidious position, for, quite naturally, everyone who quarrelled with the reigning monarch turned to the heir, and Elizabeth was acutely conscious that she must never appear as the figurehead of opposition to her sister's rule. It was for this very reason that when she became Queen herself she would never acknowledge her successor to the throne, for this represented political suicide.

'No one can fail to suppose she is a Queen'

The enmity between Catherine of Aragon and Anne Boleyn was now resumed in the next generation. Mary could never hide her jealousy of Elizabeth, which stemmed from long before her birth, when Mary was told that King Henry was intending to cast aside her mother. Despite the long periods they had been forced to spend in each other's company at Hatfield and Hunsdon, the half-sisters had little in common, and the difference in age put Mary in another generation. Half Spanish by birth, she was to marry a Spaniard and devote herself to the restoration of Roman Catholicism, which had been banished from England when King Henry had rejected her mother. Differences in religious outlook between Queen and Princess became marked right from Mary's accession. Elizabeth stoutly refused to go to Mass, and when her sister tried to teach her the error of her ways she defended herself by saying she had been brought up quite differently from the Queen and knew nothing about 'the doctrine of ancient religion'. When she at last agreed to go to chapel with her, she first pretended to be sick and then 'complained loudly all the way that her stomach ached'. Elizabeth's attendance at chapel was erratic by design and the devout Mary, desperate to see her converted, could not feel sure that she was being honest; 'she only went to Mass out of hypocrisy', she blurted out, and all her household were heretics. Some of Mary's confidants wanted Elizabeth excluded from the succession because of her heresies and illegitimacy, character- istics, they said, 'in which she resembled her mother, and as her mother had caused great trouble in the kingdom', so, too,

27

would Elizabeth. As yet there was nothing to justify extreme measures against her and when, just before Christmas, she asked permission to leave court for her home at Ashridge it was readily granted. She felt relieved to be away from Mary's side and at twenty looked forward to the first measure of independence she had known.

Fearful of the coming marriage to Philip, desperate men plotted to depose Mary and set Elizabeth to rule in her stead. It was the fact that Philip was a Spaniard, rather than his Catholic orthodoxy, that alarmed true-born Englishmen. He was the ruler of not only Spain but also the Netherlands, Milan and the New World, and therefore threatened to swallow England's identity and traditional liberties in his huge empire. Moreover, Philip demanded autocratic power for himself and it seemed that, once he had acquired the Crown, he would desert England and exploit its resources for his own purposes. Some of the ringleaders visited Elizabeth at Ashridge, others wrote, but she was far too careful to put anything in writing, though they used her name freely because of its great popular appeal. A series of regional revolts was planned, but in the end the rebels panicked into premature action in a single rising under Sir Thomas Wyatt, the son of the Tudor poet, in Kent in January 1554, which nearly cost Elizabeth her life.

'Proud, haughty and defiant'

Mary had reproved her sister for not writing to her, and now received a letter from Ashridge saying that Elizabeth had a feverish cold, more severe than she had ever experienced. The next day Wyatt raised his standard and Mary summoned Elizabeth to St James's to be under her own eyes, but she ignored the order, pleading she was too ill to move. The Queen readily believed the rumours that Ashridge was ready for a siege and that her sister was in touch with both Wyatt and the French ambassador. When the rebel army which had threatened London had been crushed, Lord William Howard and other Councillors were sent with two doctors to discover how ill the Princess really was. Although her body was badly swollen, she was not in danger and they reported she could be moved to London by easy stages – no more than eight miles a day in a litter. Her servants feared she was going to her doom and Elizabeth sent a note to Mary asking for rooms in Whitehall rather further from the river than on her last visit. At last when

28

she came to the City she pulled back the curtains on both sides of her litter so that she could be seen – a Princess, dressed completely in white, very pale from her illness, yet still 'proud, haughty and defiant'. At Whitehall Palace she remained in close custody for four long weeks, while the confessions of the rebels were sifted to try to make out a case that she was implicated in their treason, but Mary refused to see her.

At his trial Wyatt admitted writing to Elizabeth but said her verbal reply to his messenger was non-committal; after torture he signed a statement implicating her in the rising, hoping thereby to save himself, yet on the scaffold he made a categorical denial. The evidence against the Princess was too vague, but Mary remained highly suspicious and ordered her to be sent to the Tower. When she implored to be taken in front of the Queen to clear her name, the Councillors refused, but one of

Thomas Wyatt the Younger, who led a rebellion against Mary in January 1554. Defeated and imprisoned, under torture, he signed a statement implicating Elizabeth. This, however, he denied on the scaffold.

29

If any euer did try this olde sayinge that a kinges worde was more tha
a nother mas othe I most humbly beseche your. M. to verefie it in
me and to remeber your last promis and my last demaunde that I
be not codemned without answer, wiche it semes that now I am for
that without cause proued I am by your counsel frome you comanded
to go vnto the tower a place more wonted for a false traitor, tha a tru
subiect wiche thogh I knowe I deserue it not, yet in the face of
al this realme aperes that it is proued wiche I pray god I may dye the
shamefullist dethe that euer any died afore I may mene any suche
thinge and to this present hower I protest afor God (who shal iudge
my trueth) whatsoeuer malice shal denis) that I neuer practised
conciled nor cosented to any thinge that mioth be preiudicial
to your parson any way or daungerous to the state by any
mene and therfor I humbly beseche your maiestie to let
me answer afore your selfe and not suffer me to trust your
counselors yea and that afore I go to the tower (if it
be possible) if not afor I be further codemned howbeit I
trust assuredly your highnes wyl giue me leue to do it afor
I go for that thus shamfully I may not be cried out on as now I shal be
yea and without cause let cosciens moue your hithnes to
take some bettar way with me tha to make me be codemned
in al mes sight afor my desert knowen. Also I most humbly
beseche your highnes to pardon this my boldnes wiche
innocecy procures me to do toother with hope of your natural
kindnis wiche I trust wyl not se me cast away without desert
Wiche what it is I wold desier no more of God but that you
truly knewe. Wiche thinge I thinke and beleue you shal
neuer by report knowe vnles by your selfe you hire. I haue
harde in my time of many cast away for want of comminge
to the presence of ther prince and in late days I harde my
lorde of Somerset say that if his brother had bine suffered
to speke with him he had neuer suffered but the persuasions
wer made to him so gret that he was brogth in belefe that
he coulde not liue safely if the admiral liued
and that made him giue his consent to his dethe thogh
thes parsons ar not to be copared to your. maiestie yet I
pray god as euil persuasios perswade not one suthar agaynst
the other and al for that thei haue harde false report and
not harkene to the truth knowen.

therfor ons agane with hublenes of my hart, bicause J am not
sufferd to bow the knees of my body J hubly crane to speke
with your higthnis wiche J wolde not be so bold to desier
if J knewe not my selfe most clere as J knowe my selfe most
tru. and as for the traitor Wia: he migth parauentur writ
me a lettar but on my faithe J neuer receued any from him and
as for the copie of my lettar sent to the freche kinge J pray
God cofound me eternally if euer J sent him word message
toke or lettar by any menes, and to this my trueth
J stande it my dethe.

J humbly crane but only one worde
of answer frō your selfe.

your highnes most faithful subiect that
hathe bine from the begininge, and wylbe
to my ende. Elizabeth

them, the Earl of Sussex, agreed that she could write Mary a letter, and that she would be left undisturbed until she had finished. She collected her thoughts calmly and began writing with as much humility as she could, protesting her innocence but amazed that she was to be imprisoned without evidence and without the chance of defending herself to her accusers. She could not believe that this was her own sister's doing but suggested this was a plot of some of her Council. Even now she asked to come into her presence, for the thought of the Tower made her shudder – 'a place more wonted for a false traitor than a true subject'. Movingly she called on Mary's conscience 'to take some better way with me than to make me be condemned in all men's sight before my deserts [be] known'. As for the traitor Wyatt, he might perhaps have written to her, but the letter never reached her and Mary must believe this, for if she lied or had in any way communicated with the rebels let her suffer eternal damnation.

There was no more to be said and yet the writing covered no more than a quarter of the second page. Leaving blank space would make it easy for a forger to alter the whole tone of the letter by inserting a sudden recantation so she drew eleven diagonal lines across the page, leaving just enough room for a final appeal: 'I humbly crave but only one word of answer from yourself. Your Highness's most faithful subject that hath been from the beginning and will be to my end, Elizabeth.' The effort had been enormous, but Elizabeth had achieved her immediate objective, which was not merely to write the letter, but to gain time; when she had finished, the tide on the Thames had risen too high for the barge to shoot London Bridge in safety, so her masterly delaying tactics had given her another day at Whitehall, and before the day was out Mary might have second thoughts about her.

The 'tide letter', as it is called, left Mary unmoved and she was angry with Sussex and Winchester for allowing it to be written – 'they would never have dared to do such a thing in her father's lifetime'. Next day, Palm Sunday, while Mary was taking part in a religious procession, Elizabeth went on her cheerless journey to the Tower by barge. It was raining hard and the river was running high as she stepped ashore at the water-gate of the Tower, not yet called 'Traitor's Gate', through which both her mother and Thomas Seymour had passed on their way to the block. Elizabeth was afraid she would be kept in the Tower without trial for years or perhaps murdered like the Yorkist princes, Edward v and his brother Richard. 'Oh Lord! I never thought to have come here as a prisoner; and I pray you all good friends and fellows, bear me witness that I come in no traitor, but as true a woman to the Queen's Majesty as any is now living, and thereon will I take my death.' It was a courageous speech, and she went on to reprove the Lieutenant of the Tower for having soldiers to escort her. Sussex, who admired her spirit, gave out that the door of her room in the Bell Tower was to remain unlocked 'for she is a King's daughter and the Queen's Majesty's sister'. Here she remained for nearly two months, deprived of books, unable to write, with no visitor except her doctor and no chance of finding out what was happening in the world outside.

Mary could not decide what to do with her sister. There was no evidence to send her for trial, yet she could not let her return to court. Certainly she must be out of the way when Philip came to England, or she would be a rallying-point for all the opponents of the Spanish marriage. Detention had increased Elizabeth's already considerable popularity, and Londoners queued to hear the 'miraculous spirit in the wall' which kept silent when people cried 'God save the Queen!' yet to the cry 'God save the Lady Elizabeth!' it answered 'So be it', loud and clear. In the end Mary decided to send her to Woodstock Palace in Oxfordshire, the smallest and most distant of royal homes from London. All Elizabeth knew was that she was being moved and on the first night of her journey, which she spent at Richmond, she felt very near to death. Next day she was taken to Windsor, staying in the dean's house, and as she came into the heart of the countryside she was given a royal welcome in every village; the very sight of her passing by in her litter killed the rumours that she had been put out of the way. At High Wycombe housewives lined up to offer her cakes and wafers and at Aston the bells were rung in her honour. Mary had intended her removal to Woodstock as a retreat into disfavour, but Elizabeth had turned it into a royal progress. A final night was spent at Lord Williams's house, Rycote, at Thame, where she was treated with a kindness she never forgot, and then she

'Oh Lord! I never thought to have come here as a prisoner'

arrived at Woodstock, a palace in name only, for it was in a tumbledown state and only four rooms were thought suitable for her use. Meanwhile Hampton Court was being made ready as a honeymoon home for Philip and Mary, who had been married at Winchester on the day of Philip's landing at Southampton. Countryfolk took the rainswept wedding as an ill augury.

At Woodstock Elizabeth remained for ten months under the charge of Sir Henry Bedingfield, a Norfolk squire who had become, to his own surprise, a Privy Councillor. From the start there was a notable duel of wits. Bedingfield was a stickler for rules and, conscious of his responsibility, would do nothing without reference to the Council. The Princess's cofferer, Thomas Parry, was to see to the running of the household, but had to sleep at an inn in the town and, try as she might, Elizabeth could not have Mistress Ashley with her. Mary would not allow her to write to her and when Elizabeth said that in this case Sir Henry must write for her, he answered he had no authority to do so, and she retorted that she was under harsher treatment than 'the worst prisoner in Newgate'. In the end she got her way by sheer persistence and made Bedingfield petition the Council to mediate with the Queen, asking that she either be tried or be allowed to come to court; alternatively a few Councillors might visit her and then she would not be 'utterly desolate of all refuge in this world'. The captive Princess had good cause to envy the carefree life of the milkmaid. When she became ill, Mary at first refused her request for one of her own doctors, suggesting a local man might do well enough, but Elizabeth burst out, 'I am not minded to make any stranger privy to the state of my body', and the Queen had to agree to send Dr Owen to her. He found her face and arms much swollen from 'waterish humours' and advocated purging and bleeding, when the hot weather had passed, and a careful diet.

When the first Protestant martyrs were burnt at Smithfield, as part of Mary's divinely-inspired plan to reduce all England to Catholic orthodoxy, Elizabeth realised she must outwardly conform to Catholicism, but she dared to drag her feet for as long as possible, insisting that her chaplain read the litany and many of the prayers of the mass in English. When the Queen heard of this she insisted that Elizabeth must be content with

Philip II of Spain married Mary Tudor in 1554. Their marriage was extremely unpopular, as England was forced to follow policies in the interests of Spain. The loss of Calais in 1558 was the symbol of this unfortunate connection. Philip and Mary are shown here in a painting by Hans Eworth.

the Latin rite, as used in the Chapel Royal. The Princess now expressed horror at being in mortal sin and promised to obey Mary's precept 'with all her heart'. A foreign ambassador was quite sure she was only giving the impression she had changed her religion; 'however,' he said, 'she is too clever to get herself caught'.

At last Mary was persuaded by Philip to have her sister brought to court in the spring of 1555. The Queen thought she was pregnant and was nagged by fears, especially of dying in childbirth; she felt it important to face her ordeal reconciled with Elizabeth, while Philip wanted the question of the succession settled before he left England. In her final days at Woodstock, when she and Bedingfield had become used to each other, Elizabeth used a diamond from her ring to scratch three lines on a windowpane:

> Much suspected, by me,
> Nothing proved can be.
>   Quoth Elizabeth, prisoner.

Brought to Hampton Court, she found Mary in no hurry to receive her, though Philip was most curious to see her. Late one night she was taken by torchlight across the garden and up to the Queen's bedchamber and, falling on both knees, vowed her innocence of Wyatt's designs. Mary tried to trap her into saying that she had been wrongfully punished by being put in the Tower and sent to Woodstock, but Elizabeth answered: 'I must not say so, if it please Your Majesty, to you.' All she asked was to be regarded as a true subject from the first hours of the reign. The sisters had not seen each other for eighteen months and at last some measure of reconciliation was achieved. Tradition has it that this strained meeting was overheard by Philip from behind an arras.

For the moment Elizabeth was not to appear in public; though she could come to court whenever she chose, she preferred to go to Hertfordshire. There was a further rising in which the ringleaders were Henry Dudley and John Throckmorton, but it never got off the ground. This time, despite the eulogies of the potential rebels on the Princess – 'a truly liberal dame and nothing so uncharitable as her sister is' – she was in no danger, for Mary could not risk sending her to the Tower a second time and she refused to believe the wild tales that she was behind the plots. At Hatfield Elizabeth kept her little court, happy with her books and her music, welcoming Roger Ascham and enjoying the company of Sir Thomas Pope, her new guardian. When Philip, after a return visit to England, undertaken to persuade Mary to support the Habsburg war against France, finally left, the Queen turned towards her sister and in the summer of 1557 they were closer together than at any time since King Henry's death. The campaign against the French went badly, for Calais, the last outpost of a great Continental inheritance and the bridgehead fortress on which Henry had lavished enormous sums of money, was finally captured. For Mary, as for her subjects, the loss of Calais was a disaster of the first magnitude and she now saw that her marriage to Philip had brought her country's prestige to the lowest point within memory. Deserted by her husband, cruelly aware that she was barren, her dropsy became increasingly severe. Elizabeth waited on events, yet in the autumn of 1558 she began to take the initiative in confirming supporters in their loyalty, to counter any who would deny her her inheritance. Philip's special envoy, Count de Feria, came to St James's at the beginning of November and, calling the Council together, approved on his master's behalf the choice of Elizabeth as successor to the throne. Mary at the last gave her own assent, asking that her sister be made to promise to maintain the Catholic religion. De Feria then rode to Hatfield, intending to prove to Elizabeth that she would owe a peaceful accession to him. He was amazed at her calmness and certainty: 'She is much attached to the people and is very confident that they take her part ... she evidently has great admiration for her father and his way of doing things.'

Within the week Mary had died, and on 17 November 1558 the bells rang out to symbolise the opening of a new reign, as they were to ring on every anniversary of Elizabeth's accession, even after her death. Now, at the age of twenty-five, Elizabeth had come into her own, triumphant over all the difficulties that had plagued her since birth, and the ways in which she had overcome them had given her a marvellous training for the Crown that was hers by right.

11

The xj ladies rydynge upon paulfres followinge the Quenes lytter next the paulf

2 Elizabeth 'R' 1558-62

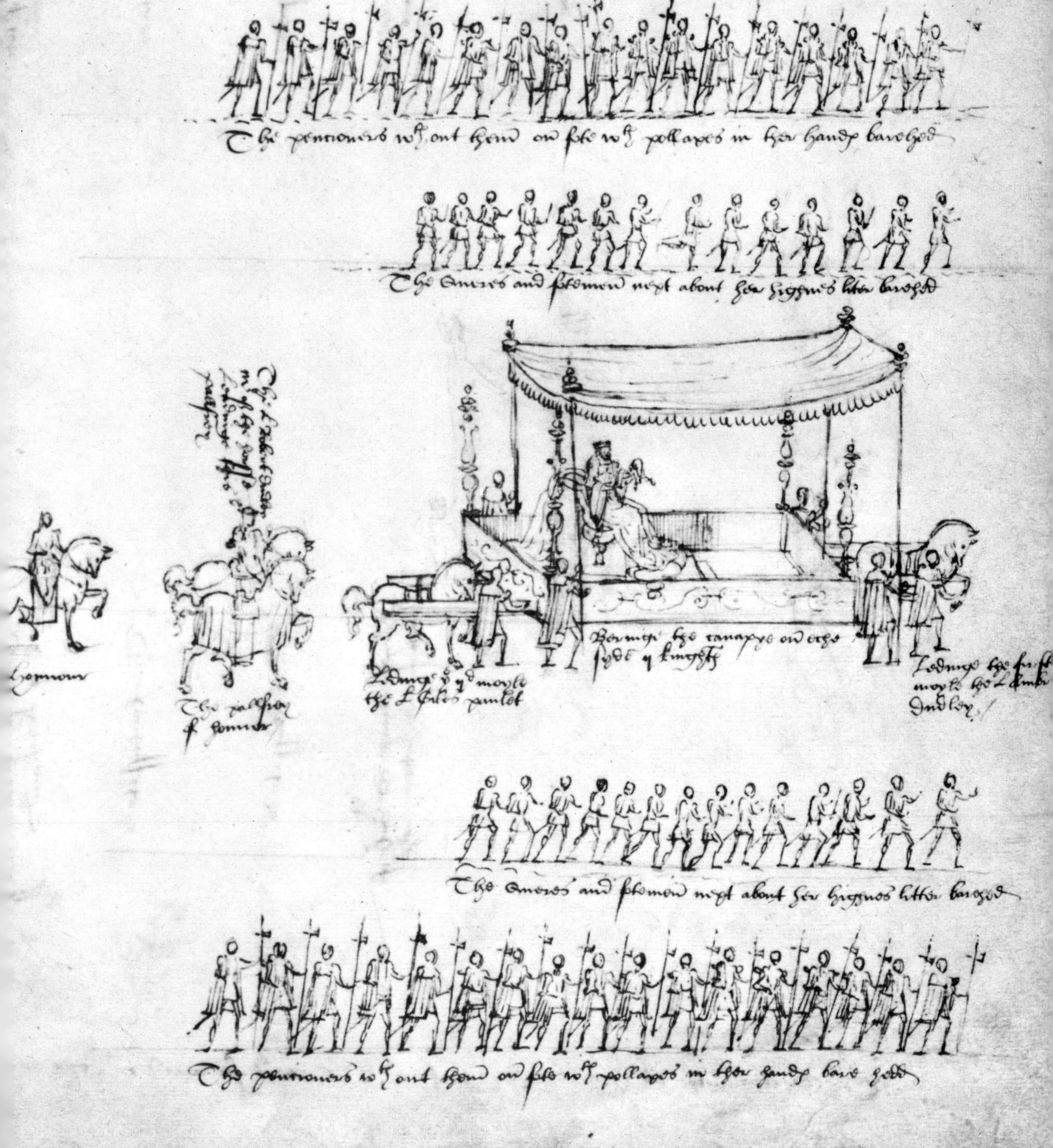

The pencioners w(i)thout there on fote w(i)th pollaxes in ther handes bareheded

The Groomes and ffotemen next about Her Highnes litter bareheded

harroun

The maister of henxes

Erles &c y(e) moste the L. Gyles partel

Borinng the canapye on evry syde q(u)ynges

Ledinge the first w(i)th the L. Chamberlen and (&)c

The Groomes and ffotemen next about Her Highnes litter bareheded

The pencioners w(i)thout there on fote w(i)th pollaxes in ther handes bare heded

THIS WAS TO BE above all an age of queens. In France the Queen Mother, Catherine de'Medici, dominated the court of her brood of sons; in Scotland Mary of Guise ruled for her daughter, the young Mary Stuart, at present married to the Dauphin of France; but it was Elizabeth of England who gave her name to the age. 'It is more to have seen Elizabeth than to have seen England', wrote a foreigner who had come under her spell for the first time, for she dazzled like a Sun Queen making her court the most resplendent in Christendom. Her name, indeed, became synonymous with England and her achievement lay in bringing up 'a nation that was almost begotten and born under her', and this in spite of being a woman.

Elizabeth was just twenty-five, tall, with her auburn hair giving her face a striking appearance. She was regal indeed in her bearing, as the coronation portrait shows; moreover, she was not at all afraid of the responsibility that was now hers after years of waiting. She enjoyed power, and would not wittingly have her prerogative clipped by Parliament or Council, for she intended to rule with no less authority than her father had done. Being Queen of England remained a vocation in itself, and she hoped to keep the 'great matter' of her marriage subordinate to it.

Although England was at war with France, hers was a peaceful accession, marked by spontaneous outbreaks of joy as the news reached out through the realm from London. Truly, in the capital there was intense relief at the passing of the old order, with the assurance that there would be no more Protestants burnt for their faith, no more subjection of England to Spanish interests. The death of Cardinal Pole, Mary's Archbishop of Canterbury, within a few hours of her own demise, heightened the break with the past; for Reginald Pole, on his mother's side a grandson of the Duke of Clarence, had urged from exile the papal crusade against Henry VIII's break with Rome. On Mary's accession he had been commissioned as legate to receive the English people back into communion with Rome. Now he was dead – not quite the last Plantagenet, but the last Cardinal to rule England. Even in the remote North Country, where Catholicism remained strong, there was an unreserved welcome for Elizabeth's accession and in York she was greeted as a Queen 'of no mingled blood of Spaniard, or

PREVIOUS PAGES
Elizabeth's coronation took place on 15 January 1559. This sketch shows the Queen being borne in her litter of yellow cloth of gold, with her coronation procession, on her way from the Tower to Westminster Abbey.

stranger, but born mere English here among us, and therefore most natural unto us'. She sensed that the vast majority of her subjects would expect her to be the very antithesis of Mary.

If it were to be a new age, the novelty would have to spring from the Queen herself, for among her advisers there were few men new to government and of those chosen many belonged to the second-generation servants of the Tudor monarchy. Elizabeth reappointed no more than eleven Privy Councillors – seven peers and four commoners – of the thirty who had served Mary, and nearly all of these had been at the hub of affairs under her father and brother. One such was the Marquess of Winchester, Lord Treasurer since 1550 and necessarily a trimmer in politics; he was now over seventy-five and was to stay in harness for another fourteen years. Elizabeth was fond of him, making fun of his grey hair and saying 'if my Lord Treasurer were but a young man I could find it in my heart to have him for a husband!' There was Henry Fitzalan, Earl of Arundel, the Lord Steward, living in her father's palace at Nonsuch, a widower of forty-seven who had political ambitions and hoped the Queen would realise he was the best match England could provide for her. Another peer retained in high office was Lord Clinton, the Admiral, an expert on military and naval affairs who sat in the Council rather as a minister of defence. Clinton had married Henry VIII's cast-off mistress Bessie Blount, long since dead, and was now husband of another remarkable beauty, Lady Elizabeth FitzGerald, the 'Fair Geraldine' of Surrey's sonnets. The Marian Councillors dismissed were all militantly Catholic in outlook, such as Lord Paget, the Secretary, and Bedingfield, Elizabeth's gaoler at Woodstock. Nicholas Heath, Archbishop of York, declined the invitation to continue as Lord Chancellor.

Of the nine new Councillors, the key appointment was Sir William Cecil, now thirty-eight, as Principal Secretary. His Welsh grandfather had fought at Bosworth with Henry Tudor, and consequently had been rewarded with a place in the King's guard and acquired property at Stamford. His father had climbed no higher though he remained a loyal, if humble, servant at Henry VIII's court and gained certain ex-monastic lands. From Stamford School, William had entered St John's, Cambridge, at a stimulating time, for he came under the influence of leading humanists – Cheke, Ascham and Thomas

'Born mere English'

41

The Queen's Men

Elizabeth's new Council in 1558 was mainly composed of men experienced in government and service to the Crown. These were to be her advisers and chief ministers for the policies of the next few years and many of them provided the Queen with long and loyal service.

LEFT Holbein's drawing of Lord Clinton, Elizabeth's Lord High Admiral. He had married two of the famous beauties of Henry VIII's court, Henry's first mistress, Elizabeth Blount, and then Lady Elizabeth Fitzgerald, the 'Fair Geraldine' of Surrey's sonnets.

RIGHT The key appointment of Principal Secretary went to William Cecil, who had served Edward VI, but was out of office under Mary. This was the beginning of a close partnership that was to last for nearly forty years.

42

ABOVE LEFT The
Marquess of Winchester,
who was Lord Treasurer
to both Edward VI and
Mary, and remained so
under Elizabeth until 1572.
ABOVE RIGHT Henry
Fitzalan, Earl of Arundel,
Elizabeth's Lord Steward.

LEFT Nicholas Bacon,
William Cecil's brother-
in-law, who was appointed
Lord Keeper in 1558.

Smith, who stood in the vanguard of Protestant truth at Edward VI's accession. Cecil left Cambridge for the Inns of Court, which he hoped would be a spring-board for preferment in the royal service. He had entered political life as Protector Somerset's secretary, survived his downfall, and though deprived of office, had conformed under Mary. As Princess, Elizabeth entrusted him with the oversight of her estates, and had come to value his judgment and honest dealing. Elizabeth and Cecil thus began a close partnership that was to endure for another thirty-eight years. In 1558 his brother-in-law, Sir Nicholas Bacon, who shared his Protestant convictions, became Lord Keeper. Loyal friends were also rewarded: old Sir Thomas Parry became Treasurer of the Royal Household, Kate Ashley Mistress of the maids-of-honour, and Roger Ascham the Queen's Latin Secretary.

Elizabeth also rallied relatives to her support, giving her government something of the flavour of a family business. Cousin Harry Carey, the son of Anne Boleyn's elder sister, Mary, was created Baron Hunsdon and became Captain of the Gentlemen Pensioners, the sovereign's personal guard. His sister Catherine became a gentlewoman of the Privy Chamber and her husband, Sir Francis Knollys, Vice-Chamberlain of the Household. Another Boleyn relative, Sir Richard Sackville, who had a flair for finance, was brought into the Council and given responsibility for many of the arrangements for the coronation. In addition, there were the Howard cousins of the Boleyns, who dominated the peerage in 1558 in numbers, wealth and honours. The head of the house, Thomas Howard, fourth Duke of Norfolk, England's only duke at this time, was too young and inexperienced for high office, though as hereditary Earl Marshal he was prominent at the coronation; but William Lord Howard of Effingham, the great uncle of both the Queen and Norfolk, who was a sailor of repute, stayed in post as Lord Chamberlain.

After six days Elizabeth was ready to leave Hatfield for the capital with a splendid entourage, and then 'the whole of London turned out and received her with great acclamation'. She rode through the streets to take formal possession of the Tower, and then stayed in the mansion in the Strand built by Protector Somerset, until Whitehall Palace had been prepared to receive her for Christmas. Her coronation was fixed, on the advice of the astrologer John Dee, for 15 January, and the most pressing problem was to find a bishop to crown her. Eight bishoprics were vacant, besides the archbishopric of Canterbury, while the senior dignitaries – Archbishop Heath of York, and Bonner of London, White of Winchester and Tunstal of Durham – were all too alarmed at rumours of doctrinal changes in the Church to act. In the end Bishop Oglethorpe of Carlisle, who had once been chaplain to Anne of Cleves, was appointed to perform the ceremony.

As always, relatively few could witness the crowning in Westminster Abbey, yet great numbers of Londoners and others could see the state processions which were enlivened by tableaux, spectacles, speeches, recitations and singing all along the route. This colourful pageantry was provided on a sumptuous scale. On the Saturday afternoon, as Elizabeth rode in her new litter of yellow cloth of gold from the Tower, where of custom she had stayed the previous night, through the decorated streets of the City to Westminster, she won the hearts of her people as no sovereign before her. This was in complete contrast to the disastrous performance of her mother's coronation procession, at which there had been feeble applause and even jeering. Elizabeth had the rare gift of inspiring loyalty in humble folk, convincing them that their love for her was fully reciprocated. 'Be ye well assured I will stand your good Queen', she said in acknowledgment to the children's choir at Temple Bar. There was only one bizarre touch on coronation day. A magnificent blue carpet had been provided to cover the route from Westminster Hall to the Abbey door, but it was ruined by souvenir hunters who each wanted to take home a piece on which the Queen had walked. 'As Her Majesty passed, the cloth was cut by those who could get at it', wrote an eye-witness, and the young Duchess of Norfolk, who walked immediately behind the Queen in procession, had difficulty in avoiding being tripped up. This was the last coronation service to be conducted according to the Latin service of medieval times, for it took place before Parliament had met to decide on a new liturgy. The rite concluded with a sung mass, but as Bishop Oglethorpe had insisted on full Catholic ritual, Elizabeth left her place during the consecration in protest.

'Be ye well assured I will stand your good Queen'

London in 1559

Elizabeth entered her capital in triumph in January 1559. She stayed at the Tower on the eve of her coronation and then travelled through the City of London and into the City of Westminster. The Queen was crowned in the Abbey and then held her coronation feast in Westminster Hall, the most ancient part of the Palace of Westminster.

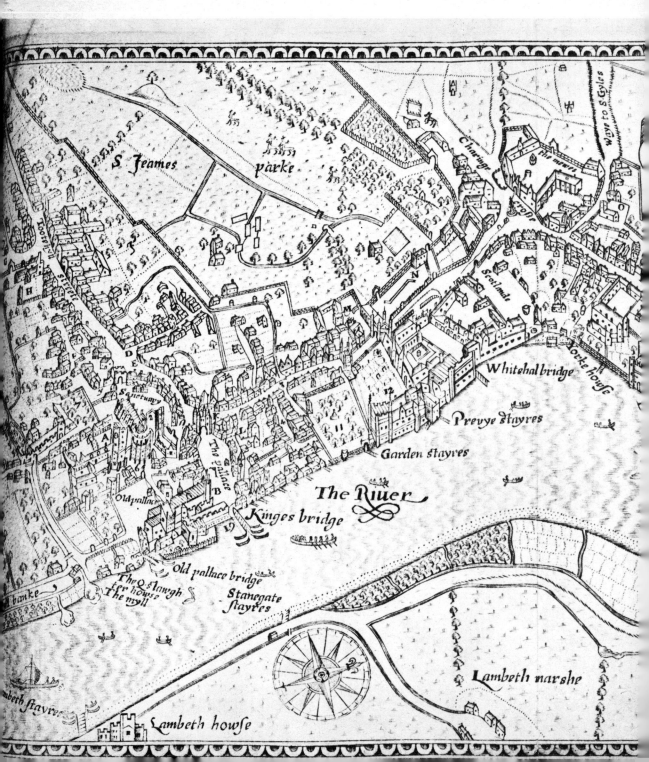

TOP Westminster Palace drawn by van Wyngaerde. The Palace and surrounding buildings huddle around Henry III's great Gothic Abbey.

ABOVE London Bridge in about 1575, from a contemporary print. (Bodleian Ms Douce 363 f.47).

LEFT Late sixteenth-century map of the City of Westminster, showing the palaces of Whitehall and Westminster, and the Strand. Along the Strand can be seen the town houses of the nobility – Somerset House, where Elizabeth stayed in 1558 until Whitehall was prepared.

47

After the lengthy service she changed from her Parliament robe into a dress of violet velvet and sat down at 3 p.m. to her coronation banquet in Westminster Hall which, with a masque and other festivities, lasted until 1 a.m. During the banquet Sir Edward Dymoke, the Queen's Champion, rode into the Hall fully armed to throw down the gauntlet and do battle against any who might dispute the Queen's legal right to her throne. None dared accept his challenge, yet Elizabeth did not under-estimate the power of those who would claim she was no true queen, despite the anointing, crowning and homage. Already Mary of Scotland, puppet of the House of Guise in France, was quartering the arms of England with her own, and there were other claimants nearer home.

The court revelled in banquets, masqued dances and plays for another ten days so that everyone had soon forgotten the gloomy last months of the old Queen's reign, and this was a welcome holiday before Parliament met and the problems of government began in earnest.

The religious issue naturally dominated the meeting of the first Parliament of the reign. The Queen saw it as her mission to heal the divisions rending the nation, and the enforcement of a general religious conformity was for her a necessary step towards national unity. It was time to call a halt to the doctrinal disputes that had been crippling England since before her father's death. His search for a satisfactory doctrinal position following the breach with Rome had ended in reaction, a Catholicism without the Pope, when there were series of heresy hunts, though Henry had attempted to hold a balance between the moderate reformers led by Archbishop Cranmer, and the conservatives led by Stephen Gardiner. On Edward's accession, England had become a Protestant state, with Cranmer's English Prayer Book of 1549, though three years later this was revised to embody a doctrinal shift to the left. With Mary came a counter-revolution – the re-establishment of Catholicism and the return of England to papal obedience. Elizabeth decided that, in place of the extreme Protestantism of her brother's reign or the rigid Catholicism of her sister's, she would keep to the middle ground, making her Church so comprehensive in its theology that there would be room in its

The coronation portrait of Elizabeth, showing her in her formal coronation robes, holding the sceptre and orb. This portrait became the standard pattern for official images of the Queen.

many mansions for all her subjects. For her the Church was the nation in its religious aspect – an establishment which she must govern by right of being Queen; her father truly was 'supreme head' of the Church and she insisted on having the same powers as he had enjoyed, although as a woman she was content with the title 'supreme governor'. Elizabeth felt deeply about religion in a non-sectarian sense, but her approach to matters over which men and women had gone to the stake was coloured by wider, political considerations. In a later Parliament, in 1566, she reminded her bishops: 'It is said I am no divine. Indeed, I studied nothing but divinity until I came to the Crown; and then I gave myself to the study of that which was meet for government.' Her Church settlement, accordingly, was an exercise in the art of the possible and, if it lacked shining idealism, it nevertheless put an end to the burning of Protestants at Smithfield and saved England from the prolonged civil warfare that had wracked Germany and would soon tear apart both France and the Netherlands. To some her 'golden mean' seemed 'a leaden mediocrity', but there was a virtue in compromise that on occasions reached idealistic heights. Conformity was all, but belief itself was a most personal matter and Elizabeth had no wish, as she put it, to open windows in men's souls.

The Church established by the 1559 Acts of Supremacy and Uniformity and enshrined in the New Prayer Book was intended to satisfy the spiritual needs of the vast majority of subjects, all in fact but the extreme wings of Catholicism and Protestantism whose tenets were anathema to the Queen. The Act of Uniformity required all subjects to worship regularly according to the rites of a broad, established Church, and there were fines for non-attendance. Those who held public offices and taught in university or school were required to take oaths of allegiance and furnish certificates that they had taken the sacrament of Holy Communion. Dissent was outlawed in theory, though providing subjects made minimal attendances at church, where there were prayers for the Queen, the government would not look too closely into their presence at the proscribed Calvinist meetings or Catholic masses. Elizabeth could never forgive the Roman Church for branding her as a bastard or for burning her godfather Cranmer, and Mary's close identification with Catholicism necessarily increased her sister's disapproval of its teaching and practice. At the same time, though she had been nurtured in the New Learning, she could not abide the sectarian iconoclasm of the men who had found salvation in the words of Calvin and Zwingli; many who had fled abroad to Geneva and Zurich under Mary returned hoping to effect a new Reformation that would replace the royal supremacy and the bishops by a presbyterian system. To Archbishop Matthew Parker's prayer 'God keep us from such a visitation as John Knox had attempted in Scotland', Elizabeth said a fervent 'Amen', for the strength of the extremists in the 1559 Parliament, when the settlement was being forged, dismayed her and she was sharp with the strongly Protestant Sir Francis Knollys for the new-fangled ideas he had imbibed from the Continental reformers. He and his fellows returning from exile, clamouring for a radical change, felt the Queen had let them down, for they never appreciated that their partisanship could endanger unity.

'God keep us from such a visitation'

For Elizabeth it was important to have the services in a language people understood, with a liturgy shaped by the Scriptures, as Cranmer's Edwardian Prayer Books had been, yet with doctrine firmly based on the historic traditions of Western Christianity. On certain matters the Queen held decided views. She was against the clergy marrying, she was suspicious of *extempore* prayer, impatient of religious disputations, and she preferred parishioners to listen to readings from the authorised Book of Homilies instead of being preached sermons by their ministers, since these could too easily lead to the spread of false doctrine. As a ceremonialist she liked the customary ritual, with her bishops and deans wearing copes and other clergy in surplices; Knollys, her Vice-Chamberlain, plagued the Archbishop without success to do something 'about the enormities in the Queen's chapel', instancing the crucifix on the altar which he felt was a mark of popery. Indeed, a foreigner reported that there was little difference between the ceremonies at Westminster Abbey and those of the Church of Rome. As a lover of music she had little regard for the congregational singing of metrical psalms, in which the men who looked to Geneva for inspiration delighted; instead her spirit was moved by the motets of Thomas Tallis and William Byrd, successive directors of the music in her Chapel Royal.

Under the strain of politics the settlement of the Church was to be found wanting, yet the Supreme Governor held to her ideal of a comprehensive Church, for there was nothing that could safely take its place. The State was too fragile to survive a radical nonconformity whether from the right or the left. A 'state within a state', with Church members owing allegiance to an external authority, whether to the Pope or to presbyterian elders, could only lead to political disruption. Thus, though no one could predict it in 1559, Elizabeth would discover that her religious policy produced martyrs in Dutch Anabaptists and Catholic seminarists – martyrs because their sin of nonconformity, which she would have forgiven, was compounded with the crime of treason, which was unpardonable.

Everyone assumed that Elizabeth would soon marry and mother an heir to the throne, so the question of the succession was regarded as secondary to the Queen's marriage. As a Princess, there had been no shortage of candidates from the Continent, including the Habsburg Archduke Ferdinand, the Duke of Savoy and the Crown Prince of Sweden. Now as Queen she was free to make her own choice and no one expected her to stay single for long.

Immediately on her accession, Philip II of Spain had ordered his envoy, Count de Feria, to press his suit, making plain that he was 'a good and true brother who really wishes her well'. Elizabeth was tactful with the Count, who was amazed that she did not seize on Philip as the most eligible man available, and who was soon out of his depth with this 'young lass' who lacked prudence. At their fourth interview she spoke frankly; she had no wish to marry anyone as yet and while she valued his King's friendship she was sure their mutual interests could be safeguarded without marriage. Her subjects were against her making a match with a foreigner and she teased the ambassador by telling him Philip would just come over for the wedding and leave immediately afterwards for Spain, as he had done with Mary. No, it was impossible for her to marry him for she was a 'heretic' (she spoke the word with evident pride) and she could never acknowledge the Pope's authority to give him the dispensation to marry her which he said was essential. The King of Spain accepted this refusal as final, and at once began bargain-

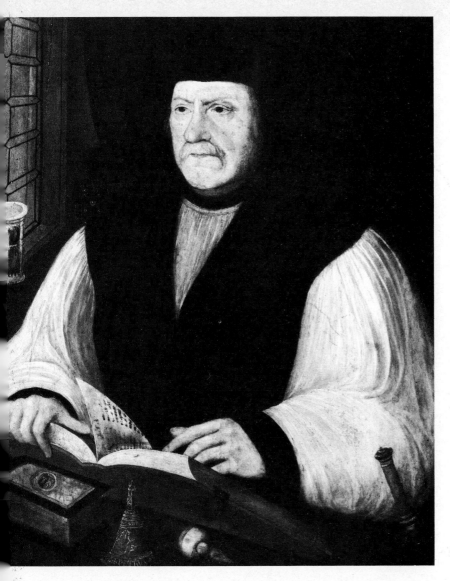

Matthew Parker, Elizabeth's first Archbishop of Canterbury. His 'middle road' policy and mistrust of extreme religious views made him a primate in whom Elizabeth could repose great confidence.

ing – successfully – for the hand of a French princess, Elizabeth of Valois. His ambassador in London was instead to canvass the merits of Philip's cousins, the Austrian Archdukes Ferdinand and Charles.

Ferdinand, though 'high-spirited and lusty', was found to be too militantly orthodox in religion for there to be any point in opening negotiations; from what she heard, said Elizabeth, he was only fit for praying for his own family. His brother Charles, the younger son of the Holy Roman Emperor Ferdinand I, seemed worth pursuing and the Queen commanded discreet enquiries to be made about him. Did he ride superbly and dance well? It was no good her being offered a man 'who sits at home all day among the cinders'. The Archduke's chamberlain came over to England to discuss the possibilities of a marriage, but Elizabeth wanted a sight of Charles himself. She asked the English ambassador in Augsburg to provide further information about his physique, complexion, habits, education, religious views and 'whether he hath been noted to have loved any woman, and in what sort'. The results were unhelpful and in the autumn of 1559 Elizabeth wrote a diplomatic letter to tell the Emperor she had no intention of marrying as yet, though she was conscious of the honour paid to her by Charles, who seemed the best possible husband for her. 'God will direct the future', she wrote, leaving the door ajar for future approaches.

The same autumn another proxy suitor arrived, to plead the cause of Prince Eric of Sweden, who had been writing most passionate love letters in Latin. Her 'most loving Eric' was bound to her eternally, he said, but as he still did not know whether she reciprocated his intense feelings he had sent his brother, Duke John of Finland, to obtain a happy answer. Duke John kept forcing his company on the Queen, scattering money and drinking freely. Splendid comedy ensued while the Swedish and Austrian envoys were 'courting at a most marvellous rate', slandering each other and threatening murder. Elizabeth soon tired of their flattery, and took care to see the two men did not meet in the palace in case they should draw swords in her presence. The Crown Prince could not believe that he was being turned down, so he summoned his brother home, accusing him of philandering with Elizabeth himself. He still held out hopes for a further two years, sending lavish gifts and vowing he would brave the North Sea to lay his heart at her feet, but he never came and finally married one of his subjects, Karin the nut girl, a soldier's daughter.

The House of Commons had been bold enough to discuss the question of royal matrimony in February 1559 and sent a loyal address, asking Elizabeth to marry. In her reply she assured her faithful Commons, that had so irritated her by raising this issue, that if she decided to marry she would never sacrifice national and religious interests by her choice of spouse, as her sister had

Philip II of Spain. He sent over to Elizabeth his envoy, the Count de Feria, to press his suit with this official portrait. The Count could not understand why Elizabeth refused to accept her brother-in-law, not appreciating how unpopular Mary's marriage to Philip had been.

done. Characteristically she left the matter vague; if she stayed single, arrangements would be made by God's help to settle the succession on a worthy heir, 'and in the end, this shall be for me sufficient that a marble stone shall declare that a Queen, having reigned such a time, lived and died a virgin'. Very few who heard those words believed she would remain a spinster, for an unmarried monarch was unheard of, and, as if their prayers were being answered, there were signs enough that she was attracted to two Englishmen concurrently. The first was Lord Robert Dudley, Master of the Horse, who by April had established himself as her favourite, and their special relationship was destined to endure, despite a multitude of misunderstandings, down to his death in 1588; the other was Sir William Pickering, a diplomat, whom she had forgotten after six months.

Pickering had been friendly with the poet Henry Howard, Earl of Surrey, before being sent on embassies. A bachelor of forty-three, he was handsome and proud of his reputation as a ladies' man. He had been ill in Flanders at Elizabeth's accession, but once he came to court he swept all before him. The Queen saw him in private – a rare privilege – and bets were being laid on him becoming Prince Consort; he spent a fortune with his tailor and acted the courtier's role in the manner born, though his bumptious behaviour upset not a few. When the Earl of Arundel, with the authority of Lord Steward, stopped him from entering the Privy Chamber, reminding Pickering that the place for knights was the Presence Chamber, not the inner apartments, he replied that he knew the rule well enough, but Arundel was 'an impudent, discourteous knave', and crossed the threshold. Elizabeth was amused by his company, but had not the slightest intention of marrying him. Before he faded from court he teased the Spanish ambassador, who was ardently singing the praises of the Archduke Charles, that he was wasting his time, for 'he knew she meant to die a maid'.

The Dudley family had enjoyed a somewhat chequered history under the Tudors. Robert's grandfather, Edmund, had been executed in 1509 for his financial extortions during Henry VII's reign. His father, John Dudley, Duke of Northumberland, rose to power after Protector Somerset's fall in Edward VI's reign. However, his attempt to secure a Protestant succession on Edward's death by marrying the Lady Jane Grey to his son

Guildford Dudley failed, and John Dudley was executed alongside his son and the tragic 'Queen' Jane.

Robert Dudley, who was the fifth son of John Dudley, had been born the year before Elizabeth, and at seventeen, in 1550, had married Amy Robsart from Syderstone in Norfolk. But for this marriage, it might well have been Robert, instead of his younger brother Guildford, who was married to Lady Jane Grey in 1553. Amy was still alive in April 1559, when Robert began to monopolise Elizabeth's company, and this invited most unfavourable comment. Although Lord Robert had been rehabilitated by Queen Mary after effective service in the French war, he was still regarded with intense suspicion because of his ancestry. Elizabeth had at once appointed him Master of the Horse – although excluding him from the Council – yet too many peers regarded him as a *parvenu*, ambitious and unprincipled. Though he built up a powerful following in the country and at court, he was never popular and made many enemies, who distorted his masculinity that had won him his unique place with Elizabeth into a vicious trait, so that in all their tales he featured as a lewd, compulsive adulterer. 'Beware of the gipsy', groaned the Earl of Sussex on his deathbed in 1582, 'for he will be too hard for you all. You know not the beast as well as I do.' Dudley remained an outsize character.

For all the appeal of this strikingly handsome man and the common belief that if the sickly Lady Dudley died Elizabeth would marry him, the friendship was only platonic in 1559. Perhaps the real attraction of the affair for the Queen lay in the assurance that she could never surrender herself while Amy Robsart was still alive. In some strange way Lord Robert hit the right note with her, treating her as a woman as well as a sovereign and charming her by his manners and conversation when she was in a relaxed mood. The people who retailed slanderous stories in Paris and Brussels about their relationship were both foolish and ridiculous if they could not distinguish between innocent flirtation and unbounded passion. When Kate Ashley, of all people, implored Elizabeth to silence the evil rumours by marrying Dudley (though she did not suggest how he was to become free to marry), Elizabeth defended herself by insisting that their relations were entirely above-board, for she was always well-chaperoned by her ladies and

56

Lord Robert was a man of honour; and yet if 'she ever had the will or had found pleasure in such a dishonourable life (from which God preserve her) she did not know of anyone who could forbid her'. In the summer of 1560 the Queen and her favourite spent days shut up together, happily ignoring state affairs. 'Not a man in England but cries out at the top of his voice this fellow is ruining the country with his vanity.' Even Secretary Cecil considered resigning and muttered that Dudley would be better in paradise than in the Privy Chamber. Then, in September, Amy Robsart was found with a broken neck at the foot of the staircase at Cumnor House.

Dudley was with the Queen at Windsor when the news arrived and she sent him away from court until the coroner's inquest was over. Eighteen months of malicious gossip put her, as well as Lord Robert, under suspicion, and gloom pervaded the palace for some weeks. A verdict of accidental death was brought in, for the evidence was not in dispute; Lady Dudley had died from a broken neck in an empty house. Her poor state of health was well known, but it was impossible for the coroner to link her malady of the breast with a broken neck, so that while Lord Robert was cleared by the law, he remained morally under a cloud. (Only recently has a satisfactory explanation been offered for the mystery of Amy's death, since it has been established medically that cancer of the breast in an advanced stage can cause a spontaneous fracture of the spine.) The manner of her end made all the difference for Elizabeth; had Amy died peaceably in her sleep, leaving her husband free from all suspicion, the way would have been open for Elizabeth to marry him after a discreet period of mourning, but circumstances made the future imponderable. The tense situation was not unlike the atmosphere in Scotland, six years later, in the aftermath of Rizzio's murder.

Marriage or no, Elizabeth felt lost without Dudley at her side and to demonstrate his return to favour she decided to create him an earl. When the warrant was brought for her signature, however, she had second thoughts and cut it in shreds, telling him for all to hear that the Dudleys had been traitors for three generations. But time was a great healer; in due course she was to make him Earl of Leicester. Despite his enemies at court, Dudley had emerged from the tragedy at

'You know not the beast as well as I do'

57

Cumnor in an even more assured position. At Midsummer 1561 he gave a water carnival on the Thames in Elizabeth's honour and she invited Bishop de Quadra, the Spanish ambassador, into her barge. In fun, Dudley suggested that since the bishop was with them he should perform their marriage that very minute, and the Queen elaborated the joke by doubting whether the Spaniard had sufficient English for the task. It was a different world from the previous September.

The Queen's failure to marry and provide an heir was brought dramatically home in October 1562 when she became critically ill with a high fever at Hampton Court. She had caught smallpox, although, because the rash was slow to appear, it was some days before the illness was diagnosed. Her usual doctors could do nothing for her but Hunsdon, her cousin, sent for the German Dr Burcot; when he told her the nature of her fever, she had him thrown out of her room. There seemed slender chance of her pulling through, but somebody took the timely responsibility of recalling Burcot to her bedside. He wrapped her in blankets, except for one hand, in which he put a bottle of 'a comfortable potion', and soon when the spots appeared her temperature fell. Lady Sydney nursed her devotedly and herself caught the infection, which left her face so disfigured that she retired from court to a life of seclusion.

During this crisis, while ministers waited anxiously, predicting the fate of England if the thread of this one life should snap, we are told there were 'nearly as many different opinions' about the succession 'as there were councillors present'. There were four principal claimants, none of whom Elizabeth would recognise, for all, however reluctant, were in her eyes potential traitors. Her own experience in her sister's reign had taught her the lesson that an heir presumptive bred faction; once she acknowledged the right of a successor she would, she said, be back in the Tower 'within a month'. The Stuart claim, which stemmed from Henry VIII's elder sister, Margaret Queen of Scotland, she regarded with much suspicion since it was the most plausible. Mary Queen of Scots, the only child of James V and Mary of Guise, had married the Dauphin who, in July 1559, became King Francis II of France for seventeen months, and on his death Mary returned to her Scottish realm. From the first days of Elizabeth's reign Mary had claimed not merely to

Frances Sydney, Countess
of Sussex, a portrait by
Steven van der Meulen.
She was the sister of
Sir Henry Sydney, and
aunt of Sir Philip. Her
husband, Thomas
Radcliffe, Earl of Sussex,
was Leicester's chief
opponent at court. She
died in 1589, leaving
£5000 for erecting a
college at Cambridge, now
called Sidney Sussex
College.

be heir but to be rightful Queen of England in her stead. In Scotland during Mary's absence, the Lords of the Congregation, inspired by John Knox, deposed the regent Mary of Guise and with difficulty persuaded Elizabeth to send an army to expel the French in what was characteristically called 'the War of the Insignia', because Mary had been using the arms of England. In the Treaty of Edinburgh, signed in July 1560, which protected England from a renewal of the 'Auld Alliance', the Scots recognised Elizabeth's right to her throne and undertook that Mary Stuart should relinquish her claim, but Mary subsequently stated she would only ratify the treaty if Elizabeth recognised her as her successor.

A second Stuart claimant was Lady Margaret Douglas, Countess of Lennox, the only child of Queen Margaret of Scotland's marriage to the Earl of Angus. Lady Margaret in turn had married Matthew, Earl of Lennox, himself a claimant to the Scottish throne, yet it was in Yorkshire that the Countess lived with her son Lord Darnley, whose English birth, according to some, made his claim to the English throne more acceptable than Mary's.

In contrast to the Catholic Stuarts, there were claimants in the Protestant 'Suffolk' line which sprang from the second marriage of Henry VIII's younger sister, Mary, with Charles Brandon, Duke of Suffolk. Her daughter Frances, married to Henry Grey, had three daughters – Jane, Catherine and Mary Grey. On Lady Jane Grey's execution in 1554 the Suffolk claim passed to her sisters, whom Queen Elizabeth kept under her eye at court, though not strictly enough, for at the end of 1560 Catherine had secretly married Edward Seymour, Earl of Hertford, Protector Somerset's son. Very few were privy to the match until the following August, when Catherine was in her eighth month of pregnancy. Elizabeth sent her to the Tower and there she gave birth to a son. Her sister Lady Mary Grey stayed on at court as a maid-of-honour and in 1565 was herself rash enough to contract a marriage without royal permission – and far beneath her, for her husband was Thomas Keyes, the serjeant porter. The couple were at once parted and banished, so they never met again. The Queen was exceptionally harsh with the Grey sisters, because she feared them as a focus of opposition.

There were two other claimants: Lady Margaret Strange, first cousin to the Grey sisters, who was thought much more suitable because her branch of the family had been unscathed by Northumberland's conspiracy; she had married Henry Stanley, heir to the earldom of Derby. The final claimant was Henry Hastings, Earl of Huntingdon, who was descended on his father's side from Edward III and on his mother's from the Duke of Clarence. The 'Puritan Earl', as he was called from his strong Protestant convictions, had married Dudley's sister. He remained a most loyal servant of the Queen who, as he told Dudley, would sometimes give his wife 'a privy nip especially concerning myself' when she came to court – a playful warning not to be ambitious on account of his Plantagenet blood.

Nothing about the succession was clear cut. In those dark hours at Hampton when the Queen was believed to be dying, Dudley naturally canvassed the claims of his brother-in-law of Huntingdon, Cecil so far as we know was among those preferring Lady Catherine Grey, while Winchester wanted the Stuart Lady Margaret Douglas or her son, Darnley; but no one spoke up for Mary Queen of Scots. Elizabeth's first words on recovering were to tell the Councillors around her bed that in case of emergency they were to make Lord Robert Dudley Protector with a suitable title and an income of £20,000 a year. A few days later she at last appointed him to the Council and, to balance him, Cecil managed to persuade her to add Norfolk's name. The unsolved problems of the succession and the Queen's marriage were understandably to overshadow all else when Parliament met again in January 1563. Just before the sessions opened, Dean Nowell of St Paul's boldly devoted a sermon to these very topics in front of the Queen. She must not delay matrimony a moment longer for the security of the realm, for spinsterhood, however virtuous in itself, was no state for a sovereign lady. 'If your parents had been of your mind, where had you been then?' asked the Dean, and it was noticed that the Queen did not answer him although she so often interrupted preachers whose words displeased her.

'If your parents had been of your mind, where had you been then?'

61

3
The
Enigmatic
Years
1562-8

Between her illness in the autumn of 1562 and the outbreak of the Northern Rebellion seven years later Elizabeth seemed to be the height of enigma; devoid of policy she extemporised with great skill, giving 'answers answerless' to the petitions of Parliament and the requests of Council on the great issues of the day, consistent only in her maddening caprice of playing for time. This was a trait born of her experiences as Princess, when she dared not appear straightforward, and as Queen she found it an invaluable course of action. Nevertheless in a crisis she was to be no slave to indecision, though the effort always cost her dearly. Every little success she achieved with delaying tactics made indecision on major problems more attractive to her. Her attitude to marriage and to the succession, her relations with the Queen of Scots and with Dudley were unfathomable and she was as isolated from her ministers as England itself was isolated in Europe. Some ascribed her unpredictable nature to feminine weakness, yet late in the reign Sir Robert Cecil was to be nearer the mark when he summed up his sovereign's character in a neat epigram: she was 'more than a man and (in troth) sometimes less than a woman'. Yet in these enigmatic years, three decades before Cecil made his remark, there were still the unresolved conflicts between the woman and the ruler.

The Commons' petition to marry and settle the succession, Elizabeth said, was a weighty matter and, being a woman, might cause her bashfulness, but she had not forgotten her people's security, even though the previous autumn 'death possessed almost every joint of me'. She side-tracked the issue by saying that though after she had gone her subjects would have 'many stepdames, yet shall you never have a more natural mother than I mean to be'. When the House of Lords sent a deputation with a similar plea she was short with them. The marks on her face were not wrinkles but pits of smallpox, and if, as some of them thought, she was an old maid (she was still only twenty-nine) God would send her children as he did to St Elizabeth. At the end of the sessions the Lord Keeper read her masterly speech which contrived to leave all the questions unanswered. Parliament was not to worry about a royal successor until all chance of having children of her own had gone; as for marriage, a personal matter if ever there was one, the time was not at present ripe for making an announcement.

PREVIOUS PAGES Hunting scene from a table carpet made in the late sixteenth century in England.

64

To attempt an escape from the dilemma she had already come to an ingenious solution, which was that her own Dudley should marry the widowed Queen of Scots. The sacrifice of losing her favourite to a rival would be almost intolerable, yet the benefits would be enormous, for Mary would be prevented from contracting a foreign match that might prove no less threatening to England than her first marriage to Francis II of France. As a reward for having Dudley as consort, Elizabeth would recognise Mary and her issue by him as successors to the throne. In a way it was only carrying a stage further her idea of making him Lord Protector if she should suddenly die. Such a scheme would free her from the buffeting of Parliament and stop her from feeling she must at all costs take a husband, especially since this might rush her into an unsuitable match with a foreigner. That Elizabeth first whispered this suggestion to the Scottish Secretary Maitland on a visit to Whitehall in March 1563 shows quite clearly that she had concluded by then that she would never marry Dudley herself; for him to reign as consort in Edinburgh with the right of succession at Westminster was the next best thing. Negotiations would not be easy, for the personal feelings of both Mary and Dudley were unknown, but to make him more acceptable in Mary's eyes she created him Earl of Leicester at Michaelmas 1564, while Sir James Melville, Mary's special envoy, was at court. The favourite's elevation, so long postponed, was to be a grand occasion and even old Winchester, who had hoped to be excused attendance, was told he must come. During the investiture, when she placed the mantle round her Robin's shoulders, she could not help tickling his neck.

Elizabeth gathered that Mary undervalued the qualities of the new Earl and told Melville that she herself esteemed him 'as her brother and best friend, whom she could have herself married had she ever minded to have taken a husband. But being determined to end her life in virginity, she wished that the Queen her sister might marry him'. The Scot paid Leicester a suitable compliment, but Elizabeth detected that he, and his Queen, thought more of Lord Darnley, who was prominent at the investiture, and more or less said so; it was as much as Melville could do to protest that no woman of spirit would prefer a beardless boy to a distinguished courtier, and yet Mary

Queen's Bench plea roll, Easter term, 1584; illumination on first membrane showing Elizabeth enthroned in the initial letter.

had instructed him to see Lady Lennox, Darnley's mother, secretly. When Elizabeth had refused to allow Mary to travel through England on her return from France to Scotland to bring pressure on her to ratify the Treaty of Edinburgh, she had perhaps inflicted a wound that was never to heal. Plans for a meeting between the two Queens were always being called off and necessarily increased misunderstanding; as for Mary, the idea of being asked to marry a passed-on favourite seemed degrading.

Queen Elizabeth's virginals. The case of Italian work bears the arms of the Boleyn family.

Elizabeth's views about Mary were second-hand. During Melville's visit she tried to extract as much information about her rival as she could, while creating a firm impression for him to convey to his mistress. She asked him which of the two Queens had the finer hair or the better complexion, which was the more skilled musician, the better dancer and the more proficient linguist. Sir James was the soul of tact: Elizabeth 'was the finest Queen in England and mine the finest Queen in Scotland'. But when he pronounced Mary to be the taller of the two she retorted: 'Then she is too high, for I myself am neither too high nor too low.' She allowed the Scot to eavesdrop on her playing the virginals, for by arrangement Hunsdon took him to a gallery where he could hear her practising alone, and then he tip-toed through a curtained door to stand behind her; aware of his presence, she stopped abruptly, pretending as if to hit the intruder and saying she was not used to perform in front of men but played for her own satisfaction, 'to shun melancholy'. He could but admit that her playing outshone Mary's. One day she took him to her bed-chamber and from a cabinet took out a little parcel labelled 'My Lord's picture' and unwrapped it to disclose coyly a miniature of Leicester, which she kissed. Melville asked if he could take it back to Mary, but Elizabeth refused, for it was, she said, the only portrait she had of him. But all her possessions, like her much treasured ruby the size of a tennis ball, would one day come to Mary if she would only follow her cousin's counsel. In the subsequent negotiations it was brought home to the Scottish envoys that Elizabeth would 'never willingly consent' to any of her subjects except Leicester becoming Mary's husband, but this did not wean Mary from her designs on Darnley. She asked that he might pay a short visit to join his father in Scotland and, although Elizabeth at

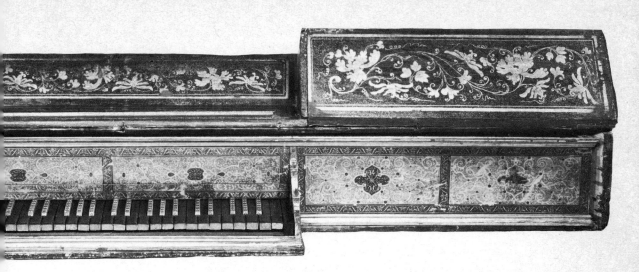

first refused permission, she later gave way at Leicester's special pleading. The Earl was afraid that Mary might suddenly become converted to the idea of marrying him and he had no wish to be banished to Edinburgh while there was still a chance of his marrying Elizabeth. Thus he used his considerable influence with the Queen to allow Darnley to travel north to his fate, well knowing what was in store for him.

Darnley had no sooner left than Elizabeth realised the folly of letting him go, so she delivered Mary an ultimatum through Randolph, her ambassador: if she would marry Leicester then her title to the English succession would be favourably considered, though Elizabeth would not hold a full enquiry into her claim until she had herself married or finally decided to stay single. Mary wept at hearing this, since she had already been captivated by Darnley, 'the lustiest and best-proportioned long man' she had ever set eyes on. As a last desperate gesture Elizabeth summoned her Councillors and had them sign a declaration that a marriage between Mary and Darnley would prejudice relations between the two kingdoms and that their Queen offered Mary a free choice of *any other* peer of her realm for a husband. It was a waste of words, as was the command for Darnley to return to court on his allegiance, for the bird had flown for good, and in a temper Elizabeth sent Lady Lennox to the Tower. In July 1565 Darnley was proclaimed King of Scotland and next day married Mary. All too soon she realised she was tied to a miserable companion, for they had few

67

THES BE TH SONES OF H RIGHT HONERABLES FERLLE OF LENOXE AD
TE LADY MARGAPETZ GRACE COVNTYES OF LENOXE AD ANGWYSE

1563

CHARLLES STEWARDE   HENRY STEWARDE LORD DAR⸱
HIS BROTHER, ÆTATIS, 6,   LEY AND DOWGLAS ÆTATIS 17

interests in common; Darnley lacked charm as well as brains and pertinacity, and before long showed his true nature as a hard-drinking boor.

If Mary's marriage brought home to Elizabeth the fact that at thirty-two she was still single, the birth of a Scottish prince the following June emphasised that she had left the question of the succession to her own throne as open as it ever had been. Her remark that 'the Queen of Scots was mother of a fair son, while she was but a barren stock' is probably apochryphal, though it sums up what must have been in everyone's minds. About this time Leicester told the French ambassador: 'I really believe that the Queen will never marry. I have known her since she was eight years of age, better than any man in the world. From that time she has always invariably declared that she would remain unmarried.' It is odd that the ambassador did not ask him why, if he believed what he said, he should have wasted the best years of his life wooing her; but the Earl, to rationalise his extra-ordinary position, added that if Elizabeth were to change her mind he would be her choice, 'for I am as high in her favour as ever'. But soon Leicester was perturbed about the renewed negotiations with the Archduke Charles of Austria, which Cecil and Norfolk had never ceased advocating. For the Queen to make a Habsburg marriage would end England's isolation, prevent any fresh threats from France and Scotland, and increase Elizabeth's standing in Europe; and since Charles was a younger son there was no danger of England becoming a junior partner in the marriage alliance.

After a slow start the subject was broached with the new Holy Roman Emperor, Maximilian II, who sent a special ambassador, Adam Zwetkovich, to discover how serious Elizabeth's intentions were; Charles would be prepared to woo the great Queen, wrote his Imperial brother, if there was some hope of a marriage treaty, but he would not, as in the previous round of match-making, 'suffer himself to be led by the nose'. Zwetkovich saw the Queen at Whitsun 1565 and delighted her by saying how eager the Archduke was to come to England and she told him that her subjects expected the marriage to be concluded. Then, as if to dash the ambassador's hopes, she added in a confidential tone: 'I have never said hitherto to anybody that I would not marry the Earl of Leicester.' Mention of Leicester

Henry Stuart, Lord Darnley, with his younger brother, Charles. Darnley was the son of Margaret Douglas, the niece of Henry VIII, so that he had a close claim to the English throne. In 1565, Elizabeth permitted him to travel up to Scotland to visit his father. By July he had married her cousin, Mary Queen of Scots, thus uniting two claims to the throne.

69

prompted her to vindicate her reputation against the slanders of the first years of her reign, in case Charles should have thought there was any truth in them, and the ambassador later made his own discreet enquiries to conclude that 'she had truly and verily been praised and extolled for her virginal and royal honour and that nothing can be said against her'. As for Leicester, she regarded him as a brother – 'in most chaste and honest love' – and there was no hope of him becoming King Consort.

The Earl, had Zwetkovich known it, was working hard to wreck the Habsburg match by intriguing with the French ambassador whom, he persuaded, could best prevent an Anglo-Imperial alliance by supporting his own suit. But Elizabeth had a nose for backstairs diplomacy of this nature and somewhat icily told the Frenchman that the very thought of marriage was repugnant to her, as it was as if someone were tearing her heart from her body. In August she and Leicester had a flaming row; she blamed him for Darnley's journey to Scotland and resented his dealings with the French. 'If you think to rule here', she shouted at him for all the court to hear, 'I will take a course to see you forthcoming. I will have here but one mistress and no master.' Her unease was intensified by the death of her much-loved Kate Ashley. To teach Leicester a lesson, and find other consolation, she took up with young Thomas Heneage of the Privy Chamber who had a pedigree of devoted service to the Tudors, for his uncle had served in Henry VIII's Privy Chamber, and had for a time been close to Anne Boleyn. Leicester, deciding this was a game that two could play, made advances to Lettice Knollys, Viscountess Hereford, 'one of the best-looking ladies of the court'. This was to develop into a passionate affair, but he had only embarked on it to make Elizabeth jealous, and he underlined this by asking for leave 'to go to stay at my own place, as other men'. After tears there was a re-conciliation, but Leicester felt life could never be quite the same again.

Surprisingly Heneage, like Sir Christopher Hatton in his turn, succeeded in achieving cordial relations with Leicester. The warm friendship of the three men in later years was remarkable; perhaps they were too close to each other to keep up personal feuds on the score of the Queen's favour and their devotion to

The Archduke Charles of Austria, the brother of the Holy Roman Emperor, Maximilian II. In 1565 negotiations were re-opened for a possible marriage between Elizabeth and the Archduke, but they foundered on Charles's religious orthodoxy. Four years later Charles married his niece, the Duchess of Bavaria.

CAROLVS·D·G·ARCHIDVX·AVSTRIÆ·DVX·BVRGVNDIÆ·STIRIÆ·CARINTHIÆ·ZC·COMES·TIROLI·ET·GORITIÆ·ZC·M·D·LXXVI

71

her remained a powerful bond as they grew older. An intruder in this charmed circle was 'Black Tom' Butler, Earl of Ormonde, who came to court in 1565 for a spell, as an interlude in a lifetime spent fighting the Desmonds and O'Neils in Ireland. His Irish charm delighted Elizabeth but, as with Pickering six years earlier, she only sought his company because he amused her. At this time Secretary Cecil set on paper the benefits that he felt would accrue from the Queen marrying the Archduke, whose suit proceeded at a snail's pace, and pithily wrote on the other side 'reasons against the Earl of Leicester'. If Elizabeth married the latter she would gain nothing, for his wealth, power and reputation all sprang from her, and he would do nothing in Cecil's view, except promote his friends and make enemies: 'He is infamed by the death of his wife. He is far in debt. He is like to prove unkind, or jealous, of the Queen's Majesty.' For him Leicester had always been the prime trouble-maker, and would hold this role until the Queen married someone else.

'He is infamed by the death of his wife'

Dislike of the Earl had not diminished. Until 1565 the most outspoken opponent had been Norfolk, who always regarded Leicester as an upstart. Each resented the other having been sworn a Privy Councillor on the same day. An example of their perennial feuding was the incident in the tennis court, when Leicester, perspiring from the play, seized the Queen's handkerchief from her hands to wipe his face. The Duke swore he would 'lay his racket upon his face' for his supreme insolence but found to his dismay that Elizabeth's anger was directed at him. Their animosity was increased by the return to court of Thomas Radcliffe, the Earl of Sussex, from Ireland, who shared Norfolk's opinion of the favourite (for his mother was a Howard, although his family had not been ennobled until Henry VIII's reign), but he was a much shrewder politician and more forceful personality than the Duke. It was difficult to remain neutral, and dangerous factions formed behind the rival earls, who armed their followers. Norfolk spoke frankly to the Queen about pursuing vigorously the negotiations in Vienna, and reminded Leicester of his promise to cease his wooing. But Leicester abandoned nothing and in the New Year seemed as sure of himself as ever, issuing all his followers with blue laces, to wear as 'party favours', and overawe the court with a show

72

of his strength, which Norfolk countered by getting his supporters to wear yellow. When pressed about his motives in opposing the Habsburg match Leicester equivocally answered that he would gladly lend his influence to the Archduke's affair, if the Queen could be brought to realise that he was not neglecting his own suit from distaste of her, since this might 'cause her womanlike to undo him'. But when through the good offices of de Silva, the Spanish ambassador, Elizabeth was approached she was no less equivocal, for she praised Leicester's unselfishness in urging her to marry for the sake of the realm, of herself and even of himself, because the Earl was always being blamed for her being single.

Elizabeth awaited detailed reports on the Archduke Charles which a fresh envoy was gathering abroad. As a man he was found to be 'beautiful and well faced, well shaped, small in the waist and well and broad-breasted; he seems in his clothes well-thighed and well legged'. Though he stooped slightly he was certainly not round-shouldered, for it was a marvel to see how straight he sat in the saddle. His manner was courteous, affable and liberal and he displayed a good memory. The only note of caution came from the Emperor Maximilian II, who hoped that his brother could be permitted to worship as a Roman Catholic, the faith in which he had been nurtured. The portrait of Charles certainly pleased Elizabeth, but, remembering her father's sad experience with Anne of Cleves, she sat on the fence until she had actually seen him.

Meanwhile the Parliament, which had been prorogued since 1563, was due to reassemble in October 1566 to vote further taxes and all her ministers feared trouble, for men from the boroughs and shires would want to know what steps the Queen had taken to marry and settle the succession. To clear the air Norfolk was delegated by his fellows to tackle the Queen at the Council table, and she was furious. Her Councillors, she told them, knew she had governed well, but the question of who should succeed her was one she would never delegate to anyone; did they wish to see her 'buried alive' by the very act of naming a successor? It was ridiculous of them to nag her about marrying because they were well aware that she was treating with the Archduke. She swept out of the room.

It was a bad start to the sessions, and worse was to come, for

Elizabeth enjoyed hunting and falconry throughout her life. As late as 1600 it was recorded: 'Her Majesty is well and excellently disposed to hunting, for every second day she is on horse-back and continues sport long.'

ABOVE Sixteenth-century table carpet showing various types of hunting.

RIGHT Elizabeth and her falconers flying their hawks at herons, from Turberville's *Book of Falconerie*, 1575.

LEFT Woodcut of Elizabeth being offered the hunting knife by her huntsman to make the ceremonial incision at the kill.

the Commons refused to vote supplies until she gave an assurance about the succession. She turned for sympathy to the Spanish ambassador, telling him she did not know 'what those devils wanted', though she knew very well that they were aiming at her prerogative. Then the Lords sent their deputation, led by old Winchester, but she told them she would only do what pleased her, for their bills could not become law without her assent. Grudgingly she said she would consult with lawyers about the succession: 'it was no business of Parliament which was too feeble-minded to discuss so weighty an issue.' Next day Lords and Commons presented a united front, with Norfolk as spokesman, but she called him a traitor; Pembroke dared to remind her the Duke was only doing his duty for the good of the country, and she swore that he talked like a swaggering soldier. Even Leicester was rapped. She had expected him to stand by her if all the world abandoned her; nonplussed he answered he was ready to die at her feet – a protestation, she sneered, 'that had nothing to do with the matter'. Before she left the Presence Chamber she ordered Leicester and Pembroke to consider themselves under house arrest.

Public business was at a standstill. Then Elizabeth decided to address thirty members from each house to scotch a further rebellious petition; Mr Speaker was debarred from attending, for she was to be the only speaker that day. With consummate skill she began by underlining her 'mere Englishry' and defended the record of her government. She promised them she would marry as soon as she conveniently could and looked forward to having children, 'otherwise I would never marry'. But now she rebuked them for discussing the succession, censoring them for not thinking about her own safety.

> A strange thing that the foot should direct the head in so weighty a cause ... I am sure there was not one of them that ever was a second person, as I have been ... There were occasions at that time I stood in danger of my life, my sister was so incensed against me; I did differ from her in religion and I was sought for divers ways. And so shall never be my successor.

She dismissed them on a more emotional note:

> As for my own part, I care not for death; for all men are mortal. And though I be a woman, yet I have as good a courage, answerable

76

to my place, as ever my father had. I am your anointed Queen. I will never be by violence constrained to do anything. I thank God I am endued with such qualities that if I were turned out of the realm in my petticoat, I were able to live in any place in Christendom.

The Commons still defied her order not to discuss the succession and then she gave way, to encourage them to get on with the subsidy bill, and even remitted a third of the taxation originally asked for. They were jubilant about this, and went so far as to incorporate in the preamble to the subsidy bill her promise to marry and settle the succession, but the Queen would have none of their revolutionary tactics and won them round. There was further trouble before the dissolution, as the vociferous Puritan group of MP.s held up other government measures while they put forward private bills to effect a root and branch reform of the Church, as dangerous a business as their toying with the succession. When finally they crowded into the Lords to hear her closing speech, she warned them and their successors never to tempt a sovereign's patience too far; she was confident that they returned home bent on making amends for their past and so she dismissed them with her blessing. She was thankful that she would never have to face the same collection of MP.s again, for now, as in 1563, they had pressed her far too closely – a thing her father would never have stood for – and yet she had still outwitted them – which he would have applauded.

The sessions had, as her Councillors had forecast, made it important for her to follow up the proposals with the Archduke. She wrote to him to suggest a meeting; 'who knows whether the choice that other eyes have made would please', but if he felt embarrassed he could slip over to England *incognito*. There was bargaining about Charles's 'dowry', which peeved the Emperor who argued that the dowry was provided by the future wife, not the husband, though he agreed that his brother should receive a suitable income from the Imperial treasury. The preliminaries dragged on interminably, so much so that Elizabeth delighted in reproving Maximilian II; she had waited five months for a reply to her last letter and felt she was either being fooled or scorned. But the Emperor did not feel at all

'As for my own part, I care not for death'

OVERLEAF In 1567 Sussex was dispatched to Vienna to invest Maximilian II with the Order of the Garter, and also to see if his brother Charles would make the slightest concessions on religion, otherwise the match with Elizabeth would be abandoned. The investiture is commemorated in this engraving by Marcus Gheeraerts showing Maximilian fully attired in his Garter robes, followed by officials of the Order from the Garter King of Arms down to two ushers.

77

En ceste place marchent deux Gentilz hommes
Vissiers, selon leur dignité et office.

Gentleman Usher.   Gentleman Usher

Icy le Chancelier ... et le Prélat de l'ordre
vont ensemble comme chefz Officiers de cest ordre

S.r Thomas Smith K.t Principal Secretary   Robert Horne Bishop of Wi—
of State.   Chancellor.   Prelate.
1572.
He was a man of extensive learning   He returned from his retire—
skilled in Chemistry. He procured an Act   Germany on the accession
that ⅓ of the rent on College Leases   beth, was made Dean of d—
should be paid in Corn. b. 1512. d. 1577.   in 1559 & Bishop of this See
                                               d. 1580.

...rois autres officiers de l'ordie	omne	Jaretier	Du treshault, trespuissant et tresexcellent Prince
'Huissier ——— Registre ———			Maximilian par la grace de Dieu Roy dés Romains
illement vont toujours ensemble			toujours Auguste, Roy de Germanie Hungarie et Boheme
			Chevalier de tresnoble ordre de la Jaretiere.

of the Black Rod

William Day Dean of Windsor
Register
was Provost of Eton 1561.
Dean of Windsor 1572. c
in 1595. became Bishop
of Winchester where he
died in 1596.

J. Gilbert Dethick Kt.
Garter King of Arms
was first Hampnes next
Rougecroix Pursuivant
thin Richmond Herald, in
1550 was created Garter
He was an industrious
Herald, Antiquary.
b. 1503. d. 1584. Æt 81

Maximilian II. Emperor of Germany, &c. 1564
b. 1527. installed 1568. 10 Eliz. died at Ratisbon 12 Oct. 1576 Æ
He was a munificent Patron of learned Men, the greatest
Master of Languages of any Prince, if not of any man, of his
time, being able to speak no less than eight with fluency.

chastened and in a note to Charles remarked on the habit of 'our illustrious Queen' of picking her way through the threads of matrimonial diplomacy, creating delays in order to gain advantages, as he had always suspected. At long last in June 1567 Sussex left for Vienna, taking in his baggage the insignia of the Garter to invest the Emperor, and a portrait of Elizabeth as a gift for the Archduke. Sussex made little headway in the vexed problem of religion, for Maximilian felt the Queen's offer that his brother would be given some latitude for his private devotions both vague and derisory, and Charles asked to have his own private chapel for mass, with his own chaplains, as a *quid pro quo* for accompanying Elizabeth to public worship in the Chapel Royal. Sussex dared not exceed his brief and sent home for further instructions. It seemed touch and go in the Council whether the Archduke would be given the further concessions, but Leicester had worked on his hot-gospelling friends, so that Bishop Jewel inflamed Protestant hearts at St Paul's Cross to have no traffic with popery, and others were saying the Archduke was no different from that other Habsburg, Philip II, whose governor of the Netherlands had begun a reign of terror against Calvinists. Elizabeth had no intention of proceeding further without the strongest of leads from her Council, but Cecil, the chief advocate of the Habsburg match, could not muster sufficient votes to defeat Leicester, with Sussex abroad and Norfolk too ill to attend, though the latter wrote forcibly, to deny that all Protestants were like Leicester, 'making religion a cloak for every shower ... naming one thing and minding another'. Elizabeth was convinced it was time to retract, though the matrimonial troubles of Mary Queen of Scots had as much weight with her as Leicester's votes in Council; she told Sussex that though she was still anxious to invite the Archduke to England there was not the slightest chance that he could persuade her to change her mind on the religious issue. Though sweet messages continued to arrive from Charles for another three years, all hope of a Habsburg marriage was ended after seven years of fruitless diplomatic wooing. Elizabeth, now thirty-four, seemed utterly relieved and Leicester was overjoyed. When the Archduke of Austria four years later married his niece, the Duchess of Bavaria, Elizabeth felt herself insulted at being 'rejected', so we are told, in favour of a mere duchess, and vowed that had she been a man she would have challenged the Emperor himself to a duel.

While the Queen's marriage now seemed a lost cause, so that men like Cecil bewailed the lack of policy, the country was remarkably quiet, and despite her isolation England remained at peace with her neighbours. The disastrous intervention in the first of the Religious Wars in France, when an army had been sent to occupy Le Havre in 1562 ostensibly to aid the Huguenots, but in effect to try to bargain for the return of Calais, had been forgotten. In contrast to affairs in England, 1567 was a critical year in neighbouring lands, forshadowing greater turmoils to come. To impartial observers there seemed considerable merit in the Queen of England's delight in compromise and the modest demands she made in taxation from her subjects. She hoped still to govern a country that was basically united, economically strong and free from foreign intervention. In 1560 she had secured her frontiers to the north by expelling the French from Scotland, but England was essentially isolated, and Elizabeth needed to retain the friendship of Spain, but not on the terms which Philip demanded. In France a second War of Religion had broken out, with the Huguenot leader Condé laying siege to Paris, to which King Charles IX and his mother, Catherine de' Medici, had fled. In the Netherlands, where the Duchess of Parma had been unable to contain the continued opposition to Spanish rule, and had even been forced to abandon the Inquisition, the Duke of Alva, a soldier of high reputation, had been sent by Philip II as military governor with 10,000 seasoned troops to exterminate the dissidents; in his first weeks in Brussels he established the Council of Blood, a tribunal that did not belie its awful name, and had arrested the Dutch leaders Counts Egmont and Hoorn.

In Scotland the prestige of the Crown had suffered from the murder in Holyrood House of David Rizzio, Mary's Italian secretary, the favourite she had chosen once she realised Darnley's worthlessness. This was followed by the murder of King Darnley in February at Kirk-o'-Field, most probably on the Earl of Bothwell's orders, to effect more than a palace revolution. Bothwell had carried Queen Mary to Dunbar and in May returned with her to Edinburgh for their marriage

OVERLEAF
The marriage feast at Bermondsey, painted by Hoefnagel. In the foreground the guests at the wedding are entertained by musicians and prepare for the banquet. In the background can be seen the Tower of London and the area just east of the City of London.

A contemporary sketch, sent to Cecil in London, of the scene after the murder of Darnley at Kirk-o'-Field in February 1567. In the top left corner can be seen the figure of the infant James – the son of Darnley and Mary – in his cradle with the legend 'Judge and avenge my cause, O Lord'. In the centre, the quadrangle of houses next to St Mary Kirk-o'-Field with the house, in which Darnley had stayed, reduced to a heap of rubble.In the bottom left corner, the dead body of Darnley is carried away. On the top right, the figures of Darnley and his servant lie in the garden, with a chair, cloak and dagger beside them.

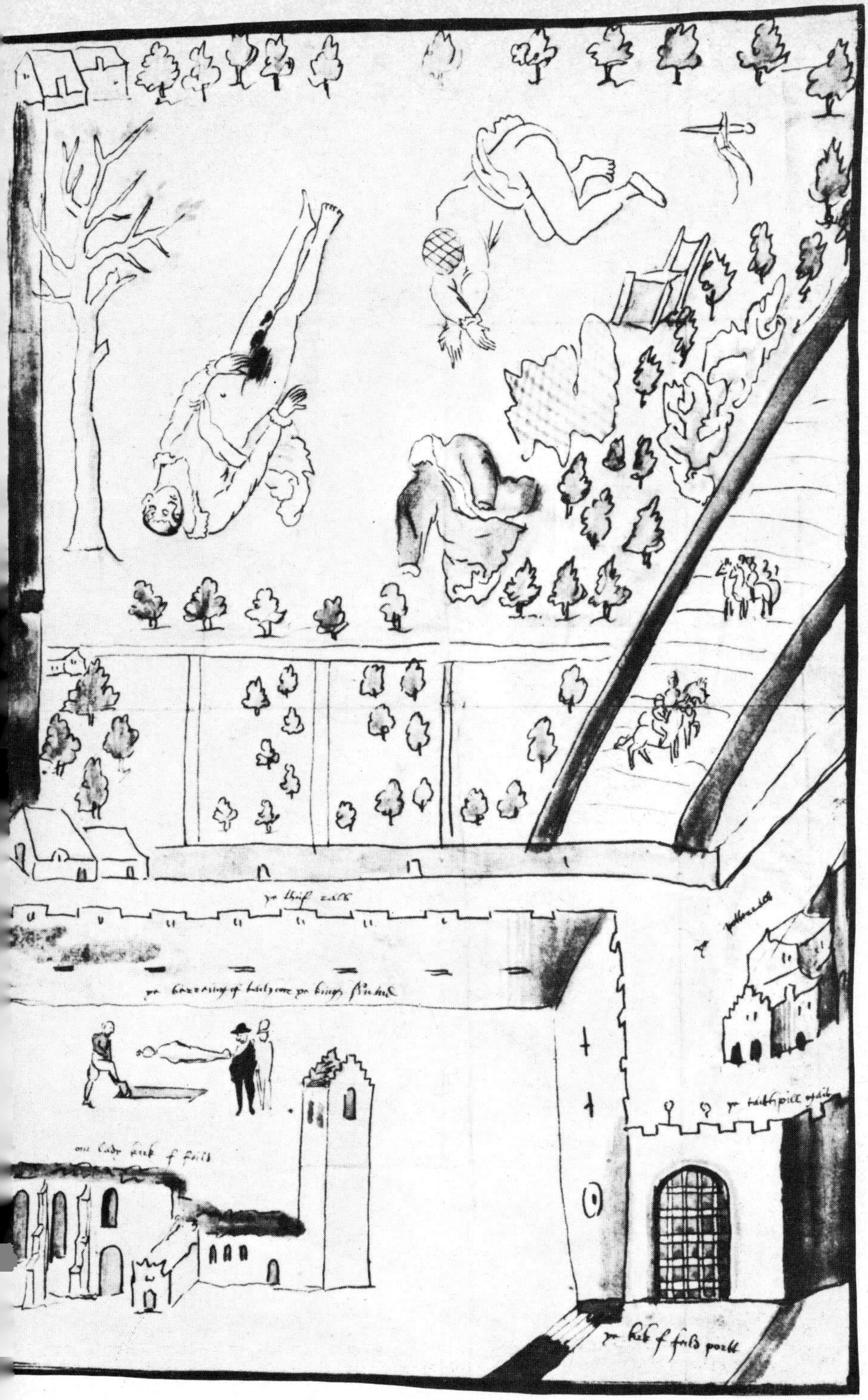

according to Protestant rites. Next month the Lords of the Covenant routed Bothwell's army at Carberry Hill and, while the Earl succeeded in fleeing, Mary was taken captive and imprisoned in Lochleven Castle. Elizabeth could scarcely credit the reports coming out of Scotland which defied any sure prediction of future events. On 24 July Mary was forced to abdicate and to appoint her step-brother, the Earl of Murray, as Regent for her son James, no more than thirteen months old, who was crowned King in Stirling Castle.

'One that has a crown can hardly persuade another to leave her crown'

Elizabeth had reiterated that the murderers of Darnley must be brought to justice, but had feared Mary had been 'looking through her fingers', for Bothwell's trial and acquittal had seemed a travesty of judicial proceedings. But the Queen's imprisonment made all the difference to her case, for Elizabeth could not allow her cousin, a Queen like herself ordained of God, to be treated thus, and she forbade her ambassador to attend young James VI's coronation. If the Lords of the Covenant dared to lay a finger on Mary's head she would wreak the most terrible vengeance on them. She promised to do her utmost to have Mary freed, to have those guilty of Darnley's death punished and to protect the person of the young King, yet in effect Elizabeth had to accept the *coup d'état* in Scotland. After eight months captivity, however, Mary succeeded in escaping from Lochleven and sent word to Whitehall asking for English aid. Her cousin congratulated her on her liberty and pledged support, if necessary, to recover her throne providing Mary did not intrigue for French aid, but before this letter arrived Mary's supporters had been roundly defeated by Murray at Langside. Prevented from reaching Dumbarton, where she had hoped to find a passage for France, Mary crossed the Solway in May 1568 and arrived in England, to throw herself on Elizabeth's mercy to afford her a refuge and subsequently to help her regain her throne. Certainly queens ruling by divine right had some obligation to translate sisterly words of affection into deeds. The one sensible remark credited to the Earl of Arundel went to the heart of the matter: 'One that has a crown can hardly persuade another to leave her crown because her subjects will not obey. It may be a new doctrine in Scotland, but it is not good to be taught in England.'

Caught up in the intricacies of Scottish politics, Elizabeth and

86

her Councillors pondered the courses open to them. To return Mary to Scotland as a prisoner would have been an unpardonable breach of faith; equally, to send an army against Murray and the Covenanters in the hope of restoring Mary by force would have broken the 1560 Treaty of Edinburgh. To allow Mary to move on to France seemed far too dangerous, for there she would be fêted as rightful Queen of England. The only practical policy was to keep her under strict surveillance in England; later she might be allowed to come to court, provided she were cleared of all suspicions in Darnley's murder. Clearly Mary's presence would encourage English Catholics in the Border Country and the North to rally to her side and to identify her with their cause, which might provoke plots and even open rebellion, so for the moment she was to be kept in Bolton Castle, a bleak fortress in Wensleydale, under the strict eyes of Sir Francis Knollys, whose strong Protestant sympathies would be an additional insurance against trouble on the score of religion. No one could predict that Mary would never leave England, and that after nineteen years as a prisoner she would be executed for high treason; no one could foresee that her flight from Scotland was the turning-point, after ten short years, of Elizabeth of England's reign, and even of her whole life. Statesmanship required her to lay aside her enigmatism.

4
Mary Stuart, the Daughter of Debate
1568-72

UNWILLINGLY ELIZABETH had found herself acting the role of arbiter between Mary and her subjects, and after sundry conversations the envoys both of the Regent Murray and of Mary herself agreed to accept the Queen's mediation. In October 1568 she appointed commissioners, led by Norfolk, who were to meet representatives of both sides at York, hearing in turn the charges brought by Mary's advisers against the Regent and the counter-charges of the infant James's commissioners against Mary, for complicity in Darnley's murder and adultery with Bothwell. The Queen of Scots had refused to appear at the York conference since she could not recognise the authority of any tribunal to try her case, yet she was willing that the Bishop of Ross, her confidential secretary, and Lord Herries should represent her. Norfolk and his fellows would not be sitting in judgment on Mary as such, and were debarred from pronouncing any sentence on her; instead they were to report their findings to Elizabeth, which would guide her in reaching a decision about Mary's future.

There was no precedent for a conference of this nature and in view of the procedural difficulties few were surprised that the men gathered at York made little progress. Murray's most telling evidence against his step-sister was the collection of letters and ballads found in 'a little coffer of silver and gilt' under Bothwell's bed. If they were genuine, these 'Casket Letters' established Mary's guilt in Darnley's murder. Murray hesitated about producing the letters, for unless he had satisfactory assurances from Elizabeth that she would in fact make a judgment on Mary, his dreadful accusation would be left in the air and, in the then state of Scottish politics, his own and his supporters' lives would be in danger. Outside the conference room, Maitland, the most skilled of the Regent's party, whispered to Norfolk that the surest way out of their quandary would be for the Duke to marry Mary himself; she could then be safely allowed to return to her throne and in the fullness of time she or their heirs would rule in England as well. A few years back, when Mary had turned down the offer of Leicester, Elizabeth had suggested Norfolk's name as a suitable consort, but Mary had been too enamoured of Darnley to give it serious thought. By 1568 the situation had completely changed and Mary, as a prisoner, was grasping at straws. Gradually, from

'A little coffer of silver and gilt'

this conversation with Maitland as they went hawking by the River Ouse, Norfolk came to fall in love with the idea. Thrice widowed, like Mary, he had not the strength of character to hold back from reaching towards so glittering an ambition; even though he was sure of the authenticity of the Casket Letters, which horrified him as he read them, he was bewitched by the thought of Mary.

Thomas Howard was by birth a 'thane of Cawdor' and he saw in marriage with Mary the opportunity to be 'King hereafter'. The son of the poet Surrey, and grandson of Henry VIII's Lord Treasurer, he was a cousin of the Queen and had persistently felt she had undervalued him. The first peer of the realm and the wealthiest landowner in the country, he perpetuated the Howard distaste for the new nobility, which had helped towards Surrey's downfall; in particular, as we have noticed, he resented Leicester's rise to favour. Aloof, every inch an aristocrat, and in his own demesne in East Anglia a king, he had not achieved the high office to which he thought birth and natural ability entitled him. Fundamentally a weak character, his ambitions led him unwittingly into high treason, though he never realised that he was compromising his loyalty to Elizabeth or to her Church, for, despite Catholic connexions, the pupil of John Foxe remained an Anglican.

Elizabeth heard enough to suspect that Norfolk had been showing undue partiality to Mary's cause at York and smelt danger; in consequence she transferred the conference to Westminster under a much enlarged body of commissioners. Here, after much shilly-shallying, the Casket Letters were produced and sworn to be authentic. Yet the Bishop of Ross refused to answer the charges, for Mary had not empowered him to do so as she did not acknowledge the tribunal competent to deal with her. In a letter Elizabeth complimented her on having so skilled an adviser as the Bishop, yet urged her to answer the charges, for if she could plainly establish her innocence she would be a free woman. All Mary would do was to plead to be allowed to come to Elizabeth and answer for herself, as the dignity of a sovereign queen demanded nothing less, but Elizabeth for her part refused to demean herself by giving an audience to one accused of murder and adultery, even if she were a royal cousin. Once again stalemate had been reached, though Elizabeth was now in a very strong position; with the evidence of the Casket Letters before her, no monarch in Europe would deny her the right to keep Mary in strict custody. Before the Westminster Conference broke up there had been further secret remarks about Norfolk's matrimonial plans. Elizabeth felt justified in asking him quite openly about these rumours, which he denied, and then asked him if in the future he might perhaps be persuaded to change his mind, if such a marriage could be shown to be for the benefit of both countries. Again came his denial; he could not possibly love one that had been 'a competitor to the Crown' and even if Elizabeth implored him to marry the Queen of Scots he would prefer banishment in the Tower, 'for he meant never to marry with such a person where he could not be sure of his pillow' (referring to Darnley's murder). Yet despite these fulsome protestations he had already made up his mind to attempt this dangerous scheme and, though he had never seen Mary, he felt already committed and that he must honour his word to her, in preference to his solemn undertaking to his own Queen. Elizabeth still questioned his loyalty, but it would have made no difference had he known this, for he had cast his die.

These were trying days for Elizabeth. For all her personal dislike of Mary, who had never abandoned her pretensions to be rightful Queen of England, she bewailed her forced abdication which was an indignity that no crowned head should be allowed to suffer. Her cousin of Norfolk had clearly deserted her, and her heart was heavy with the death of another cousin, Lady Knollys, whom – after Kate Ashley's passing – 'she loved better than all the women in the world'. Mary's arrival in England had put new spirit into the Catholics in the Northern Counties where the Earls of Northumberland and Westmorland were supreme, and, contrary to the Queen's personal wishes, the laws against recusancy were being administered with much greater severity. Relations with Spain had been jeopardised by the seizure of three ships sent by Philip II with £85,000 of treasure for paying Alva's troops in the Netherlands; these had taken refuge in Plymouth Sound in a gale, but on Cecil's advice had been impounded. English property in the Netherlands had been seized in retaliation and an embargo on trade imposed.

The year 1569 opened with an attempt by Leicester and

Norfolk to remove Cecil from the commanding position he had occupied since Elizabeth's accession. The Duke and the favourite, so long sworn enemies, made strange bedfellows. As Principal Secretary, Cecil was the instrument of policies which had become increasingly unpopular and in the framework of the Tudor constitution the 'opposition' could only attempt to unseat him by backstairs intrigue. It is fair to say that no chief minister of England after 1700 could have remained in office in the face of such criticism. Elizabeth, as usual, knew more than the plotters realised and saw their manoeuvre to secure Cecil's dismissal as an attempted *coup* against her. Some of his opponents had a personal axe to grind: to Leicester he was the man who had prevented him from marrying Elizabeth, to Norfolk he was the man whose hatred of Mary would stop at nothing. Others took their stand on political grounds, such as Northampton, who disliked Cecil's brand of Protestantism that had led to the support of Calvinists in France and the Netherlands, and to his favouring the Suffolk claim to the succession, while such staunch Catholics as Arundel regarded a change of Principal Secretary as the essential preliminary to a change in religious policy.

As with Cromwell in 1540, Cecil was to be charged with being an evil adviser in the Council room and once he was in the Tower 'means to undo him would not be far to seek'. With superb timing, however, Elizabeth called a Council herself and, when Cecil's enemies excused themselves from attendance, she took an early opportunity of scotching the plot. When a group of them were gathered in the Privy Chamber on the afternoon of Ash Wednesday, she reproved Leicester for his unbusinesslike attitude towards Council affairs and when he defended himself by shifting the blame on Cecil, who was thought by many to be ruining the country, the Queen rushed to the defence of the Secretary and roundly abused Leicester. Norfolk said to his neighbour loudly enough for all to hear: 'You see, my lord, how the Earl of Leicester is favoured as long as he supports the Secretary, but now that for good reasons he takes an opposed position, she frowns on him and wants to send him to the Tower.' Northampton replied: 'No, no, he will not go alone.' Making them all appear as whispering conspirators, Elizabeth had shown quite unmistakably that Cecil retained her full confidence and

OVERLEAF Elizabeth I being carried by her courtiers, a painting attributed to Robert Peake. This picture was probably painted in 1600, but shows the Queen as a youthful figure. The Gentlemen Pensioners line the route, and ahead of the Queen are the following Garter knights: Edmund Sheffield; Charles Howard of Effingham; George Clifford, 3rd Duke of Cumberland; Thomas Butler, 10th Earl of Ormonde; unknown; George Talbot, 7th Earl of Shrewsbury; Edward Somerset, 4th Earl of Worcester.

93

that she regarded any attack on him as an attack on her. Pouncing in this way she had taken the wind out of their sails and she hoped that would be an end of intrigue.

In the weeks which followed other plots took shape and, though they differed in scope and detail, a common factor was that Norfolk should marry Mary. The most serious plot was the plan of the Earls of Northumberland and Westmorland to raise the standard of revolt among the Northern Catholics, seize a port and invite Alva to land with an army. Family ties entered this plot, for Westmorland had married Norfolk's sister, Jane. Leicester supported the marriage proposal, for it seemed to offer a happy solution to a number of problems; once married to the Duke Mary could be restored to her throne, ratify the 1560 Treaty and be recognised as Elizabeth's heir; and since it would no longer matter whom Elizabeth married, the Earl could at last achieve his ambition. Leicester was confident he could convert a majority of the Council to his way of thinking and be able to force the Queen to approve the Duke's marriage, but the delicate negotiations must be left in his hands alone. Norfolk took the opportunity of Cecil's absence from Council to suggest to colleagues that the safest way of dealing with Mary would be to release her on condition that she married an Englishman, and those present agreed with him. Leicester undertook to inform the Queen firmly but tactfully of their resolution, yet he remained inert. Elizabeth in fact caught wind of the affair from some of her ladies, even thinking that the business had been finalised over her head, and she confronted Leicester with her wrath, though he brushed the matter aside as 'women's gossip'. Later, in the gardens at Richmond, she asked Norfolk himself what news he had for her. He pretended not to understand her question so she asked it more plainly: 'You come from London and can tell no news of a marriage?' The Duke had not the nerve to make a clean breast of it. At the start of the summer progress, when she was staying at Loseley House, near Guildford, she asked him to her dinner table and with a nip warned him to take 'a good heed to his pillow', using his own phrase, which he could not fail to understand; he was badly shaken, but fearing he might damage Leicester's plans, he said nothing. Elizabeth had given him every chance of being frank with her but as he had not responded she felt

*'Take a good heed
to your pillow'*

96

justified in believing he could no longer be trusted.

The Duke left the progress for London, thinking he could not now withdraw from his undertaking with Mary, and approved a desperate plan of Northumberland's to rescue the Scottish Queen when he should give the signal. It was Elizabeth's other cousin, Hunsdon, who now filled in the details for her. Leicester, knowing his own vulnerability, had taken to his bed at Titchfield, pretending he was ill and when Elizabeth came to comfort him he blurted out all he knew about the Norfolk-Mary marriage, craving forgiveness; his own loyalty, he said, was above reproach and, as always, she succumbed to his magic. But Norfolk was in a different category. She had summoned him from London on his allegiance and charged him with furious directness to deal no further with Mary. He bemoaned the day he had entrusted this business to Leicester, who had boasted how effectively he could handle the Queen, and now, at Titchfield, the Earl set the tone for other courtiers to treat him with icy disdain. Without permission he withdrew from court to the capital where rumours were rife – an act of defiance that seemed the prelude to a grand rebellion in which Northumberland and his fellow Catholic dissidents in the North might carry with them Elizabeth's severest critics on the Council. The danger seemed even greater when the Duke, instead of obeying a summons to repair to Windsor, made off to his country residence at Kenninghall. Those around the Queen stood in suspense, expecting the worst, and Elizabeth made plans for the immediate execution of Mary without ceremony if the Duke took the field with an army. Yet his removal from London was not a declaration of war but a cowardly retreat. When further summons came he pleaded he was too ill to travel, as Elizabeth had done in Wyatt's day, and utterly cowed he wrote to her, seeing the shadow of the Tower, which was 'too great a terror for a true man'. Finally he submitted, urging the Earls of Northumberland and Westmorland to call off their revolt, and threw himself on the Queen's mercy.

Throughout the summer the Northern Earls had been preparing for battle and could count on the blind devotion of their tenants in the feudal North Country, who regarded their liege lords with much greater loyalty than they spared for the Queen. They promised to rise as a man in defence of the old religion and to vindicate Mary's rights. The causes of their discontents were variously interpreted; as Sussex, the Lord President of the Council in the North, put it, 'some specially respect the Duke of Norfolk, some the Scottish Queen, some religion and some, perhaps, all three'. Their fathers had risen against Henry VIII with Robert Aske in the Pilgrimage of Grace when the monasteries had fallen, and now they in turn followed the hallowed banner of The Five Wounds of Christ. Sussex, who was under some suspicion because of his friendship with Norfolk, had summoned the Earls to York, but they feared a trap. The bells of Topcliffe church eleven years back had welcomed Elizabeth's accession, but now they were rung backwards as the signal for rebellion. Even at that late hour the whole campaign might have been called off had not Lady Westmorland, Norfolk's sister, shamed the leaders into action; if they did nothing now, she said, they could never again hold up their heads but creep ignominiously into holes. On 10 November the armed retinues of Percy and Neville rode into Durham and, entering the cathedral, threw down the English Bible and the 1559 Prayer Book before hearing the Roman mass. Before long a much larger army was doing the same at Ripon, for Sussex with only a sadly depleted militia at his disposal had not dared to oppose them. From Ripon the Earls issued a proclamation calling on all men to flock to them to rescue the Queen of England from evil advisers who had subverted the true faith, good policy and the ancient nobility, though they said nothing at this stage about Mary.

To Elizabeth the danger seemed very great. She had no standing army to send against the rebels and with great men's loyalty under suspicion it was only natural that she should stay in the safe fortress of Windsor with Leicester at her side. She placed complete faith in cousin Hunsdon who had rapidly collected an army of landowners and tenants from the Midlands and was marching north. Supporting forces under the veterans Clinton and Warwick included not a few who had taken up arms in the hope of being rewarded with rebels' lands when the struggle was over. Already Mary had been removed from Wingfield to Tutbury, where the Puritan Huntingdon replaced the easy-going Earl of Shrewsbury – the fourth husband of the formidable Bess of Hardwick – as her custodian, but with the

98

Henry Carey, Lord Hunsdon, Elizabeth's first cousin through his mother Mary Boleyn, Anne Boleyn's sister. He led the main army against the rebels and decisively defeated Dacre in Cumberland in February 1570.

rebels coming within striking distance of Tutbury Elizabeth ordered Huntingdon to bring Mary as far south as Coventry. With Hartlepool in rebel hands there was danger of Alva landing his professional soldiers there and papists were reckoning he could be in London by Candlemas, hearing high mass in St Paul's.

Suddenly, on 25 November when they had reached Tadcaster, the Earls decided they could not advance any further in safety, for Hunsdon's army lay to the south, so they deemed it prudent to withdraw to familiar territory to make a stand. As they made their strategic retreat northwards their supporters lost heart, and with the sharp wintry weather the ranks thinned disastrously. By mid-December in Durham City the Earls felt they

99

had no choice but to flee across the Pennines into Scotland. But the threat of Leonard Dacre in the West Marches remained. At the outbreak of the rebellion, Dacre, a Catholic still smarting under the adverse decision of the civil courts about his claim to the Dacre barony, had remained in London, but he was persuaded to ride north and strike a blow against the régime. He assembled a private army at Naworth which was too strongly fortified for Hunsdon to attack, so he made for Carlisle. Dacre followed him, however, to fight an action in the spirit of the Border Ballads, which ended in his defeat. As soon as Elizabeth heard of Hunsdon's victory she sent a formal letter of congratulation, ending with a postscript in her own hand:

> I doubt much, my Harry, whether that the victory were given me, more joyed me, or that you were by God appointed the instrument of my glory; and I assure you that for my country's good the first might suffice, but for my heart's contentation the second pleased me .... And that you may not think that you have done nothing for your profit, though you have done much for honour, I intend to make this journey somewhat to increase your livelihood, that you may not say to yourself, *perditur quod factum est ingrato*. Your loving kinswoman, Elizabeth R.

The promise was richly fulfilled and throughout the North the redistribution of the lands of Percy, Neville and Dacre to courtiers ended the separatism which the dissolution of the abbeys a generation back failed to end. In the verse she wrote to celebrate the rebels' defeat – the same poem in which Mary was termed 'the daughter of debate, that eke discord doth sow' – Elizabeth spoke of taking her rusty sword 'to poll their tops that seek such change' and in her revenge she was merciless, demanding harsher reprisals than Sussex had envisaged, so that seven hundred and fifty men were executed under martial law. Soon the Church courts were busy so that several hundred clergy, either open Catholics or crypto-Romanists, were deprived of their livings.

A hundred days after Dacre's defeat, the papal bull of Pius v was published, deposing Elizabeth and absolving her Catholic subjects from their allegiance to her. John Felton had nailed the document on the door of the Bishop of London's palace, an act of defiance that cost him his life, for the bull spoke of Elizabeth as 'being without dominion and privilege', a heretic queen who now stood 'deprived of her pretended right to the realm'. Had the bull arrived from Rome at the outset of the rebellion it might have stiffened many wavering sympathisers of the Earls, of Mary and of the Catholic faith, but by now it was a damp squib. The Queen thought Pius's action insufferably insolent, and he struck at the unity of the realm. It would be impossible now to refrain from opening windows in men's souls, for the bull forced practising Catholics into being potential traitors, since all English Catholics who continued to obey the Queen were liable to the sentence of anathema. It was answered by a repressive code of legislation against Catholics that was to last until the early nineteenth century.

Rebellion had dashed Mary's hopes of an early release; as Sir Francis Walsingham, at this time ambassador in France, wrote, 'the thirst of a kingdom can never be quenched until it hath hazarded the uttermost trial'. But Norfolk was a different case; even though Elizabeth was slow to accept her Council's

Tutbury Castle, Staffordshire, which remained Mary's prison for many years from February 1569. Here she was guarded by the Puritan Earl of Huntingdon, himself a cousin to Elizabeth.

views that he could not be charged with high treason as the law stood, she shouted at them that he could easily lose his head on her authority alone. After nine months in the Tower, he made a full confession, promising never to deal with Mary again, and was allowed to go to his own home in the Charterhouse, under house arrest, for he was still too dangerous to be at large. Here he fell under the spell of the Florentine Roberto Ridolfi, who had prepared an incredibly optimistic plan for a large-scale rebellion to rescue Mary, backed by foreign money and arms. Mary's adviser, the Bishop of Ross, gave his assent because it seemed the only chance of her becoming free. The Duke of Alva with an army was to land at Harwich to join forces with the thousands of men Norfolk was to put in the field to assassinate Elizabeth, take London and to release Mary. The Italian reckoned that nearly half the peers were Catholics at heart, who could muster not less than 39,000 men! After the suppression of the Northern Rebellion probably no more than three peers, put on their allegiance, would have sided with Alva, had he landed. Moreover, their tenants and the majority of Catholic recusants in 1571 still placed their loyalty to the Queen above that to the Pope.

Both Alva and Philip II thought the plans foolhardy and withheld promise of Spanish aid until the English Catholics should have staged a successful rising on their own resources. Norfolk still felt himself in honour bound to keep his pledge to Mary, and in his simple way drifted unwittingly into treason by signing letters to the Pope, Philip II, Mary and others, perhaps without knowing their full contents. But the conspirators were careless. Letters were discovered, cyphers broken and accomplices put on the rack revealed too much. Norfolk went back ignominiously to the Tower, but ironically Ridolfi, the arch-plotter, escaped arrest. To save himself the Bishop of Ross told all, corroborating the Duke's guilt and implicating amongst other nobles Arundel, Lumley, Southampton and Cobham. Ross even betrayed Mary whom, he said, was not fit to acquire another husband, for she had poisoned her first, Francis II, agreed to the murder of the second, married his assassin, and then led Bothwell into battle so that he might be killed. The Queen of Scots could not believe that the Bishop had deserted her thus.

My lord me thinkes that I am more beholdinge to the hinder part of my hed than wil dare trust the forwardo side of the same and therfor sent to the Levetenant and the S. as you knowe best the order to defar this execution till they here furdar and that this may be done I dowt nothinge without _ curiocitie of any furthe warrant for that her rasche determination upon a very unfit day was countermanded by your _ considerat admonition the cause that moue me to this ar not now to be expressed lest an irrevocable dide be in mene while comitted. If the wyl nides a warrant let this suffice all writen with my none hand. Your most lovinge soveraine

Elizabeth R

There were to be other plots against Elizabeth's life in later years, but the revelations of the Ridolfi conspiracy coming so soon after the Northern Rebellion, alarmed her most. That her own cousin of Norfolk, her senior peer, should have intrigued for her downfall was the cruellest blow she had yet suffered. Whom now could she trust? The mercurial Leicester had been the broker bringing together the Duke and the Scottish agents in 1569; but for that disastrous intrigue the later troubles might never have arisen, even if he had not swerved from his devotion to her since his full confession at Titchfield. There were rumours – false as it happened – that another favourite, Hatton, was not entirely reliable and that the young Earl of Oxford had devised a madcap scheme to rescue the Duke. Among the group of

Norfolk was found guilty of treason in February 1572, but Elizabeth was reluctant to send her premier peer to the block. This letter of April, to Burghley, defers the execution still further. Norfolk was finally executed on 2 June 1572. (Ms Ashmole 1729 ff. 13).

inner Councillors there were only Cecil and Bacon and her relatives Hunsdon and Knollys, whose loyalties were beyond reproach and none of the four was popular. Elizabeth felt the loneliness of her position more intensely than ever. After the verdict against Norfolk in Westminster Hall she continued to hesitate about signing his death warrant. One day, moaned Cecil, she was adamant that the law should run its course, but the next she wanted to hold back when she remembered the Duke's nearness to her in blood. The new Parliament cried out not only for Norfolk's blood but for Mary's head on a charger, too. Cecil himself knew well enough that unless he could persuade the Queen to order the Duke's execution the chances of bringing Mary to trial would be remote, and at last Elizabeth gave way. After five months delay she sent Norfolk to his death on 2 June 1572, but for many years to come the execution was to trouble her mind and she was to blame Cecil.

Even now she was angry at Parliament for its misguided concern for her own safety. She had intervened to stop the

One of the great prodigy houses of the Elizabethan age was Longleat House, Wiltshire, built by Sir John Thynne (above) largely to the designs of Robert Smythson. Thynne arose from the circle around Protector Somerset. He produced at Longleat (right) one of the first classical houses in England.

Commons from proceeding against Mary by bill of attainder (in place of a state trial) but now, when another measure passed both Houses, depriving Mary of any title to the English throne, declaring any subject who dared make the claims for her a traitor, and making her liable for trial if she were in the slightest degree connected with a further plot against Elizabeth's life, all this she vetoed and sent Parliament packing.

Taking stock of the situation in the summer of 1572 as Elizabeth approached her thirty-ninth birthday, it is surprising how little had been achieved since 1558. Those who had lauded her succession felt sadly let down. Religious unity, on which she held such store, had been shattered and England, a weak and divided country, was still without a firm friend in Europe; even relations with Spain, on which the bulk of overseas trade depended, had been severed. Against all advice Elizabeth had deliberately shirked making decisions about the succession, had deliberately made negative decisions about marriage, and on all major issues she was at odds with her Council, Parliament and

RIGHT Elizabeth, Countess of Shrewsbury (1518-1608) – known to posterity as Bess of Hardwick – was a formidable lady. In 1568 she married her fourth and wealthiest husband, the 6th Earl of Shrewsbury, who became Mary Queen of Scots' jailer. Bess quarrelled with her husband, and turned her activities to building, first at Chatsworth and then Hardwick, her last and greatest house.

RIGHT On the balustrades at Hardwick, she placed her initials – 'E S' for Elizabeth Shrewsbury. The façades are filled with wide expanses of glass, and Hardwick has been called a 'lantern' house as a result.

BELOW In the High Chamber at Hardwick, the walls are covered by decorated woodwork and tapestries below, and stucco scenes from classical mythology above.

Convocation. In April 1572 she had been seriously ill and though at first she put it down to something she had eaten, it was most likely an attack of colic, complicated by a high fever. She was convinced she was on her deathbed and for three days and nights Leicester and Cecil kept their vigil at her side. Had she not pulled through Elizabeth would have gone down in history as a supreme example of unfulfilled promise, a princess who had lacked the qualities to develop into a successful sovereign, in short a failure, and – no less than her sister Mary Tudor and her cousin Mary of Scotland – a standing warning that a monarchy could not be entrusted to a woman. Few appreciated that even then Elizabeth was the exception to any general dictum and that, whereas for most queens femininity was the prime cause of weakness in their rule, she made her sex a source of strength.

Le Duc d'alençon

5 Matrimonial Diplomacy 1572-84

THOUGH SHE LIVED in a predominantly masculine society, Elizabeth easily dominated it by evoking a remarkable emotional response from courtiers in general – not merely from the few she highly favoured – who felt moved to pay her a special kind of homage simply because she was a woman. This secular devotion was different in kind from the intense loyalty she aroused from being an anointed Queen ruling by divine right, and it owed most to the old idea of chivalry, which had kindled a deep respect for women in general and for the ideal of spotless maidenhood in particular. This 'courtesy' was evident from her first days as Queen, but over the years it developed through her own encouragement into a strong personal cult. She charmed courtiers into participating in the sophisticated idyll of the Virgin Queen and wanted to believe that each of them was a little in love with her. Praised by poets and musicians as Fair Oriana, as Cynthia the moon goddess, or as the immortal shepherdess of a moving pastorale, she lived out this mystical romance on a public stage. On her Accession Day tournament each November the gallants would break a lance for the honour of their sovereign lady. These allegorical fantasies had by no means reached their full elaboration by 1572, for most subjects still fervently hoped, and many still expected, that Elizabeth would marry.

Leicester had, as far as matrimony was concerned, remained faithful. Indeed the only thread through all the twists of his political actions since Amy Robsart's death had been his determination to pursue his royal courtship, and when not in Elizabeth's presence he sent gifts to keep his name green, and letters in which his warm affection was never stifled by stilted phrases – 'your most bounden, for ever and ever, R.D.' She now nicknamed him 'Eyes', but there was another on whom she had bestowed the name 'Lids' – Christopher Hatton.

Hatton, a Lincolnshire squire's son bred to the law, had caught Elizabeth's attention by his well-proportioned figure and skill at dancing in a masque given at one of the Inns of Court, and this had earned him a place in her personal bodyguard in 1564. It was another seven years, when he was thirty-one, before the Queen's favours towards him began suggesting to some that here was a rival to Leicester, and there were slanderous tales not so different from those that had been embroidered earlier

PREVIOUS PAGES, LEFT
Francis, Duke of Alençon, the fourth son of Henry II of France and Catherine de'Medici. He was the prince that Elizabeth so nearly married.
RIGHT Miniature of Elizabeth by Nicholas Hilliard, painted in about 1590. This picture reflects a youthful idealisation of the Queen, the expression in visual form of the poets' worship of her beauty in the last years of her reign – 'the mask of youth'.

about Lord Robert's relations with Elizabeth. Hatton, said the malicious, 'had more recourse to Her Majesty in her Privy Chamber than reason could suffice, if she were virtuous and well inclined as some noiseth her'. In 1572 she appointed him to succeed Sir Francis Knollys as Captain of the Gentlemen Pensioners, and gossip increased. Leicester, much displeased at his promotion, mocked his dancing and chided the Queen that if she wanted to see someone who really could dance divinely, he would introduce her to a certain dancing-master. 'Pish,' came the reply, 'I will not see your man; it is his *trade*.'

Sir Christopher was to crown his career by becoming Lord Chancellor at the very end of his life. Before then he had acquired a lease of the Bishop of Ely's London house, the 'Naboth's Vineyard' near Holborn he had coveted with its splendid gardens; the Hatton Garden which is today the centre of the trade in diamonds. In his native Lincolnshire he had built Holdenby House as a 'shrine' for Elizabeth to sit in, for the mansion was dedicated to her and, despite his rickety finances, he could not have her come to stay often enough.

Even when Hatton was riding on the crest of the wave he felt insecure, for besides Leicester, there were Heneage and, later, the young Earl of Oxford competing for favours. Oxford, who had been brought up in Cecil's household, had been given a rigorous education and encouraged to develop those accomplishments that Castiglione had listed as essential for a true courtier. His nimbleness as a dancer at times made even Hatton seem leaden-footed – a splendid return on all those hours of lessons at seven every morning. Elizabeth certainly delighted in his company, but he threw overboard a promising career, first by marrying Anne Cecil, his guardian's daughter, which proved a disastrously unhappy match, and then by showing how little he cared for a courtier's life by trying to enlist as a soldier of fortune in the Netherlands. Later still, he embarked on an extensive and spendthrift grand tour. Edward de Vere, Earl of Oxford, was feckless, thoughtless and a 'heel', keeping his countess short of money yet lavishly supporting indigent poets and actors. The Queen found him a most unsatisfactory favourite, yet there was something appealing in his eccentric, dissolute ways, and after anger and tears would come reconciliation. Her continued favour of this worthless aristocrat, against

Nicholas Hilliard:
the Queen's miniaturist

'... a hand, or eye
by Hilliard drawne, is
worth a history by a
worse painter made ...'
(John Donne: *The Storm*)
Hilliard was trained by the
Queen's goldsmith, and
emerged in the 1570s as the
finest miniaturist under
royal and noble patronage.
Apart from a brief
interlude of service
to the Duke of Alençon,
he worked almost entirely
for the first Elizabeth I
and then James I.
He was much influenced
by Holbein and by French
court portraiture, and his
style found particular
favour with the Queen.

RIGHT Hilliard's self-
portrait painted in 1577 at
the age of thirty, when he
was in the service of Francis
Duke of Alençon.

FAR LEFT Hilliard's famous allegorical miniature, *Young man leaning against a tree among roses*, which has been suggested might depict the Earl of Essex.

LEFT *Young man with flames*, another of Hilliard's allegorical miniatures, painted in about 1588.

ABOVE Elizabeth's Second Great Seal, made in 1584 to replace the seal which had been in use since the beginning of the reign. In July 1584 Nicholas Hilliard and Dericke Anthony, graver at the Mint, were ordered to 'embosse ... patterns for a new Great Seal according to the last pattern made upon parchment by you. Our Servant Nicholas Hilliard'. The reverse showing the Queen on horseback.

Edward de Vere, 17th Earl of Oxford, (1550-1604) one of the Queen's favourites. He was an accomplished courtier – his talent for dancing appears to have been unsurpassed, but he was also an eccentric and dissolute character, hardly living up to Castiglione's ideal.

her better judgement, was to set in train the wildly improbable story that they were lovers, and the Earl of Southampton was their offspring!

Hatton was alone among the Queen's favourites in remaining a bachelor to his death, ever hopeful that his passionate love would be returned. When he fell ill with a painful kidney complaint in 1573, Elizabeth visited him every day, and when he could travel she arranged for him to go to Spa in the Low Countries with one of her own doctors. It was this, the first absence from court in nine years, that made Hatton aware how deep was his emotional involvement with Elizabeth. In letter after letter he told her that 'to serve you is heaven, but to lack you is more than hell's torment'. Never again would illness or the fear of death make him leave her side and while for the moment there was the Channel between them she must daily remember 'Your *Lids* that are so often bathed with tears for your sake. A more wise man may seek you, but a more faithful and worthy can never have you'. Sometimes he signed his letters with two small triangles, representing 'Lids', in others he made a pun of his surname, drawing a hat, crossed through with an X ('Hat-Ten').

Of all the correspondence Elizabeth received from admiring courtiers, from the young Dudley at the beginning of the reign to the young Essex at the end, perhaps Hatton's missives alone come into the category of 'love letters' as the term is generally understood. Others were expressions of courtly gallantry, written by men who knew how Elizabeth fed on admiration and the choicest flattery that the language allowed, but Hatton's had something more potent than a mere sugary flavour; he was sure he was in love with her, and when it became clear that she would not respond to the passionate, physical love he so desperately wanted, he did not react as Leicester or Raleigh and look for fulfilment in marriage with someone else, but remained in love with the idea of being in love with her, constant, dedicating his celibate life wistfully to the dreams of what might have been. Even this was part of the masquerade of Fair Oriana. Hatton wept freely when his star was not in the ascendant and would go off and sulk in the country, anxious to find a go-between, like Heneage (who was safely married), to act as messenger to bring back the magic. There was a regular

114

succession of teasings, tiffs, retributions and reconciliations. A characteristic present which he sent to return from the shadows was a rich jewel in the shape of a true lover's knot, 'the kind she most loves, and she thinks cannot be undone' as he wrote in an accompanying note.

Though Leicester and Hatton were to become remarkably close, it was probably the Earl's jealousy at Hatton's rise that made him begin his liaison with Lady Douglas Sheffield, by birth a daughter of Lord William Howard, the Queen's great uncle. Leicester had cuckolded her husband during a royal visit to Belvoir Castle, for Lady Douglas did not reject his advances. However, she carelessly mislaid a compromising letter of Leicester's and when Lord Sheffield heard of this he set out for London to begin divorce proceedings. Before he had made any progress, however, he became ill and died in 1568, leaving a widow of twenty-four. Leicester's enemies later accused him of poisoning Lord Sheffield, but it would have been a pointless crime, for he had no intention of marrying Douglas. Five years later he was again so often in her company that 'the Queen thinketh not well of them'. There was talk that they had contracted to marry and Douglas claimed somewhat dubiously that she in fact married Leicester at Esher in 1573. Certainly she bore him a son, Robert Dudley, whom Leicester did not disown, but the father was not to be trapped into matrimony. He continued his flirtation with Frances Howard, Lady Douglas Sheffield's sister; and in the wings stood Lettice Knollys. Much was kept from the Queen so that the Earl might still pay homage as a suitor, but his relations were becoming dangerously complicated, while Hatton's were transparently simple.

Elizabeth had cautiously resumed the hobby of matrimonial diplomacy and, with the Habsburg negotiations having come to a full close, she turned to the house of Valois. She had put out feelers through Fénélon, the French ambassador, at the end of 1570 telling him if she ever needed a husband she would look for him in a royal house of similar rank to her own. Enjoying the friendly bantering which this remark provoked, she added: 'But I am an old woman and am ashamed to talk about a husband, were it not for the sake of an heir.' In a more serious vein she confessed that in the past she had been courted by some who had been more concerned to marry the kingdom than its

'To serve you is heaven, but to lack you is more than hell's torment'

Queen – 'as generally happens with the great, who marry without seeing one another'. After further audiences Fénélon tried out the suggestion that the ideal man for her was Henry of Anjou, brother of King Charles IX. His mother, Catherine de'Medici, believed tales that Elizabeth was lame, yet she would not easily allow him to miss the chance of a crown and Anjou's ultra-Catholic sympathies were played down. But Elizabeth was worried by his age. In strict confidence she asked her ladies for their views, and while Lady Clinton tactfully said that Monsieur's youth would be no obstacle because he was virtuous, Lady Cobham was painfully blunt – to marry Anjou was a charming idea, but there was always trouble between partners when there was an age-gap. 'Nonsense' answered the Queen, 'there are but ten years difference between us' (actually it was nearer twenty). She even suggested he might pay a visit *incognito*, crossing the Channel one morning to reach her for dinner outside Dover, so they could see each other for a few hours, but the Duke was little interested and jibed that she was 'not only an old creature, but had a sore leg' – words which hurt Elizabeth to the quick, and an apology from Catherine de'Medici was somewhat tardily offered.

The Queen was enjoying the preliminary negotiations and Lord Treasurer Burghley (as Cecil had become) felt sure she was now in earnest, so he warned Walsingham in Paris to play down the religious difficulties. The prize of having her married was too great to slip through the fingers and, if the match went ahead, the 'curious and dangerous question of the succession', said Burghley, could at last be buried, 'a happy funeral for England'. The special envoy sent over by Catherine de'Medici suggested as the basis for a treaty that Anjou should be crowned King the day after the wedding and rule jointly with Elizabeth; the private income demanded was not excessive, but the religious articles were – Anjou and his whole household must be allowed the free exercise of Roman Catholicism. As with the Archduke Charles in 1567, this proved the sticking-point, yet Elizabeth was anxious not to have a French courtship ended abruptly and hoped there would still be a political alliance between the two countries. Catherine suggested that where Anjou had been rigidly orthodox his younger brother, Francis Duke of Alençon, might prove 'a much less scrupulous fellow',

Catherine de'Medici, the consort of Henry II of France. On her husband's death she became regent for her sons as they successively became kings of France – Francis II, Charles IX and Henry III. Her fourth son and youngest child, Francis Duke of Alençon she sought to make consort of Elizabeth I.

so she substituted his name as the Valois candidate.

Officially Charles ix still made forceful representations about the unjust imprisonment of the Queen of Scots, but when he learnt details of Mary's part in the Ridolfi plot he knew he was wasting his breath. 'Ah, the poor fool will never cease until she loses her head', he shrewdly predicted. With the French attitude to Mary clarified, the way was open for a political agreement, and in April 1572 the two countries signed the Treaty of Blois by which each undertook to come to the aid of the other in case of attack, and France agreed to recognise the *status quo* in Scotland. At last Elizabeth had an ally in Europe and at last Elizabeth's ministers felt they could take the question of Alençon seriously. He had been christened Hercule, but Catherine had changed his name to Francis. To Elizabeth doubts on the score of religion were at this stage subordinate to doubts about the Duke's appearance and youth. Smallpox had scarred his face and he was unusually short; more alarming was the fact that the beardless boy was three years younger than Anjou, making him less than half the Queen's age. Even so, she found her talks with Alençon's personal envoy, M. Le Mole, re-assuring. Then, suddenly, came the terrible news of the Massacre of St Bartholomew, stemming from the assassination on Catherine's orders of the Huguenot leader, Coligny, in Paris. All chance of compromise in France, with some degree of religious and political toleration for Huguenots, was dashed, all hope of rule by the centre party, or 'Politiques', was gone, for power returned to the Guise faction. The Massacre opened up old wounds, plunging the country into further series of civil wars, and France became a blood-bath. As reports of the massacre in Paris reached the provinces, cities and towns held their own purges of the Huguenot community. This was a grim moment for Protestantism in Europe, for the news from France was interpreted as an evil conspiracy by the powers of the Counter-Reformation and yet, before long, it provoked greater solidarity among Protestants of different persuasions and countries than any other single event. Soon Protestant refugees were landing in the south and east coast ports and Englishmen who could understand their tales of horror swore they would go to La Rochelle and join the forces of their co-religionists.

Fortunately for Elizabeth Parliament was not sitting, or she would have been under great pressure from the Puritan wing to throw over the French alliance and terminate her dealings with Alençon. When, after a pleasurable visit to Warwickshire in Leicester's company, she had first heard of the Massacre she made Fénélon, the ambassador, wait for three days before deigning to receive him at Woodstock to learn his version of the events. To put her court into mourning, as some wanted, would have threatened the alliance which she desperately wanted to maintain, but Alençon's suit must be postponed. She agreed to stand godmother to Charles IX's baby daughter, but felt political conditions in France too dangerous to allow Leicester to represent her at the christening; the Earl of Worcester, who undertook the mission instead, met with pirates in the Channel who made off with the Queen's christening gift.

Alençon's love letters so fascinated Elizabeth that she pleaded with him to come over and see her in strict secrecy; a boat from Calais could bring him straight to the landing-stage at Greenwich where she would welcome him quite alone. Their romantic meeting was not, however, to take place for another six years. At this time the Duke was in prison for plotting with the Huguenot leaders. His mother, still ambitious for him to win a crown – like his brother Anjou, who had been elected King of Poland – and still anxious to have him settled outside France where he seemed bent on causing trouble, wondered whether Elizabeth was really interested in pursuing her irresponsible son. Elizabeth's reply was firm: she could not now think ill of a man who had spoken so highly of her, but she could not take a husband 'with irons on his feet'. He was released soon afterwards and negotiations for a marriage treaty were resumed for a few months, until the death of Charles IX altered the situation. In 1574, when the Duke of Anjou left Poland to succeed as Henry III of France, Alençon inherited the title of Anjou, though it will avoid confusion if we continue to call him Alençon. During the festivities at the French court marking the accession, Catherine de'Medici dressed two female dwarfs in English costume to mimic Elizabeth and even to jibe at her father's reputation. It was low comedy in very poor taste, and when the Queen heard about it from her envoy, Lord North, she joined in the intrigues to rescue Alençon from his domineering

The Massacre of St Bartholomew by François Dubois. This took place on 24 August 1572, as a result of Catherine de'Medici's orders that the Huguenot leader, Admiral Coligny, should be assassinated. It has been estimated that fifty thousand Protestants were killed in Paris on this day, and in the provinces in the days which followed.

mother, as a snub. Catherine eventually apologised, saying if Lord North's French had been better he would have realised that the buffoonery of the dwarfs was not at all insulting. Henry III soon married Louise of Lorraine, and Elizabeth was reassured to be told that there was 'more beauty in Your Majesty's little finger than there is any lady' at the French court, 'or in them all'. Meanwhile Alençon seemed to have forgotten her completely and was concurrently courting the daughter of Philip of Spain and a sister of Henry of Navarre.

Elizabeth relapsed into playing the role of a sovereign spinster with some relief, yet she became noticeably more embittered and her maids-of-honour resented her dog-in-the-manger attitude to marriage. Mary Shelton, who had married without

'I would not
forsake that
poor and single
state to match
with the greatest
monarch'

asking her permission, was roundly cursed and had her ears regally boxed, but she was lucky compared with Lady Bridget Manners, guilty of the like offence, whose husband was sent to prison. When Frances Vavasour, a lady-in-waiting, secretly married, the Queen was, as usual, furious and defended her fury: 'She hath always furthered any honest and honourable purposes of marriage or preferment to any of hers when, without scandal and infamy', her permission was sought in the proper manner. She would never relinquish her proprietary rights over 'any of hers', and seemed to take a sadistic pleasure in blighting the honeymoon days of runaway lovers. If marriage was being entered into simply because the lady was pregnant, or if the facts of a wedding had been kept from her right until a child were born, her anger knew no bounds. The marriage of one of her ladies or maids meant breaking up her intimate family circle and her dislike of change became overlaid with jealousy of those round her who had found happiness in matrimony. Sir John Harington, her godson, recalled that she often asked the ladies in her chamber 'if they loved to think of marriage, and the wise ones did conceal well their liking thereto, knowing the Queen's judgment in the matter'. It was to Harington that she sent a copy of her speech to Parliament in 1576 in which she confessed her dislike of marriage.

> If I were a milkmaid with a pail on my arm whereby my private person might be little set by, I would not forsake that poor and single state to match with the greatest monarch. Not that I do condemn the double knot, or judge amiss of such as, forced by necessity, cannot dispose themselves to another life; but wish that none were drawn to change but such as cannot keep honest limits.

Even so, for the sake of her good people, she would be prepared to sacrifice principles and happiness, providing the conditions were favourable. By the end of 1578 she had decided that they were, and her principles seemed in the melting pot, for she could talk of nothing but the French Duke.

The 1570s had been momentous years for the Netherlands. A fortuitous marriage had brought the Netherlands to the House of Habsburg at the end of the fifteenth century, and this Burgundian 'inheritance', with its international port of Antwerp, became the wealthiest and most strategically important of the family's possessions. With the abdication in 1555 of the Holy Roman Emperor, Charles V, the Netherlands had been apportioned to Philip II of Spain, but the men of Flanders and Holland regarded him as a foreigner, although his father, in early days proud of his title 'Charles of Ghent', had throughout his reign carefully nurtured the Netherlands, confirming their considerable privileges. Spanish autocracy cut at the heart of 'Burgundian liberties', while Philip's bigoted Catholicism put his subjects in the Northern Provinces, where Calvinism had taken root, in fear of the Inquisition. Out of the long struggle for independence against Alva and his successors developed not one, but two states – the forerunners of modern Holland and Belgium in which religious differences coalesced with linguistic. Flanders, Brabant and the Southern Provinces were Flemish-speaking and predominantly Catholic, while the people of Holland, Zeeland and the north spoke High Dutch and were Protestant. It is as though north and south had been joined by accident in the Burgundy of old, and, despite the leaders' aim of a united Netherlands, freed from Spanish tyranny, many of their compatriots in arms found too little basis for unity.

In March 1572 Elizabeth had closed English harbours to the Dutch 'Sea Beggars', who had been preying on Spanish shipping, and this decision, taken on an impulse, had far-reaching consequences. The privateers under Count la Marck, unable to stay in England, seized Brill in South Holland as a base in their own territory – an event that marks the real outbreak of the Revolt of the Netherlands against Philip II of Spain. Their expulsion had relieved Anglo-Spanish tension so that diplomatic and commercial relations, broken off since 1568, were resumed with the full understanding that each country should expel the rebels of the other. The internal troubles of the Netherlands, France, and even Scotland, were to give Elizabeth a period of security during which England could develop her strength and national consciousness. Elizabeth knew, however, that civil war in Flanders and Holland could only have disastrous effects on English trade, so she offered to mediate between Philip and his rebellious subjects. Once Alva had been replaced by Requesens as Governor of the Netherlands, she tried more persistently to bring both sides together. She blamed William, Prince of Orange, on whom the mantle of Count Egmont had fallen as the leader of the protest movement against Spanish rule, for continuing the war for the sake of a religious toleration with which she had no sympathy. William's Calvinism was no less repugnant to her than his rebelliousness and, though there were English volunteers fighting under the Dutch banner, she openly proclaimed William a rebel.

Between the death of Requesens and the arrival of his successor, Don John of Austria, in 1576, the Spanish army mutinied and sacked Antwerp. This act shook all Europe, for the city was the financial hub of the Continent. The States-General signed the Pacification of Ghent to unite all seventeen provinces, and appealed to Elizabeth to mediate with Philip to confirm the Pacification and recognise a self-governing community under Spanish sovereignty, free from military rule and religious persecution. Accordingly, Don John on reaching Brussels issued the Perpetual Edict as the only way of restoring order to the provinces, undertaking to evacuate all troops within twenty days. The Edict was, however, misnamed. Don John, the victor of the Battle of Lepanto against the Turks, had gazed in admiration at a portrait of Elizabeth, praising her for 'her virtues and mighty puissant state', yet he reckoned that the only chance for Spain to regain effective power in the Netherlands was to have England under a ruler devoted to Spanish interests – and the ambitious general reserved this role for himself. Elizabeth heard enough of his plans to insist that the Spanish soldiers leave Flanders by the overland route, for Don John had intended to embark them for England where he would rescue the Queen of Scots, marry her and rule in Elizabeth's stead. In a panic he seized Namur, while under William of Orange's leadership the States-General in Brussels deposed him and appealed to England for help. Elizabeth immediately offered them a massive loan and was soon lending money, on the security of her jewels, to enable the German prince John Casimir to lead an army of mercenaries to aid William. Puritan hotheads demanded open intervention, but the Queen dared not risk a breach with Spain. Moreover, her Alençon had now undertaken to lead an army against Don John, though in the autumn of 1578 the Spaniard died of a fever.

Catherine de'Medici had been delighted when the troublesome Alençon found a niche in the southern Netherlands, where the Catholics of Artois and Hainault had elected him 'Defender of Belgic Liberty against the Spanish tyrant'. But the prospect of even part of the Low Countries becoming French through conquest was a more serious threat to English interests than continued Spanish domination. This threat persuaded Elizabeth that she must herself control Alençon's activities, and so she revived her suit. Alençon fell for the bait, for even if he failed to become her consort he could surely ask her to become his paymaster. For the moment he sent Jean de Simier as an *aide* to woo her by proxy. Simier proved 'a most choice courtier, exquisitely skilled in love toys, pleasant conceits and court dalliances'. Such gallantry made Elizabeth feel a different woman, even if he were a proxy suitor, and she nicknamed him her 'Monkey'. She revelled in his attentions, and took a girlish delight in the escapade of his raid on her bedchamber to steal a nightcap that he could forward to Alençon as a love token.

Leicester and Hatton were put in the shade and accused Simier of using love potions. When a lady-in-waiting spoke up for Leicester, the Queen countered by asking her if she seriously thought she would so far forget her position to prefer a servant she had raised to 'the greatest prince of Christendom?'. Enchanted by Simier, she tended to forget he had only come to blaze the trail and then she felt Alençon was delaying his visit unreasonably. It was not as if he had to deal with 'a lady with some defect', she reminded her ambassador in Paris; there would be excuse for getting cold feet if he were being asked to court a sickly or ugly princess, but since the Almighty had endowed her generously, 'which we ascribe to the Giver and not glory in them as proceeding from ourselves (being no fit trumpet to set our own praises) we may in true course of modesty think ourselves worthy of as great a prince as Monsieur is'. The French wanted a definite answer, but she refused to commit herself until she had seen him. Surely outstanding clauses in the treaty could be settled personally between the two of them? At last the Duke agreed to come to her.

When Elizabeth signed Alençon's passport, Leicester took to his bed with a diplomatic illness to provoke her sympathy, for he found the idea of her marrying the Frenchman intolerable. He had been quite open about his opposition, and Simier was convinced that the guard who had tried to shoot him in the

'we may . . . think ourselves worthy of as great a prince as Monsieur is'

Family life of the wealthy

RIGHT The Cobham family, by the Master of the Countess of Warwick. The stiff formal style of the painting contrasts with the charming domesticity of the subject.

BELOW Scenes from the life of Sir Henry Unton. Unton was the son of Anne, Countess of Warwick, and she is to be seen nursing him in the bottom right-hand corner. In 1595 he visited Henry IV of France as a diplomat for Elizabeth, where he died. His body can be seen being shipped home, and being buried.

OPPOSITE Detail from the life of Sir Henry Unton, showing his wedding feast. The diners are entertained by musicians and by costumed figures taking part in a masque.

124

gardens at Greenwich was in the Earl's pay. Had Simier been a casualty, Alençon would certainly have called off his visit, and the 'Monkey' was as worried about his own safety as about the success of the discussions. He now played his strongest card, for he had succeeded in uncovering a secret that was unknown even to the Queen: Leicester had married Lettice Knollys, the widow of the Earl of Essex, in the previous September. This news he now proceeded to impart to Elizabeth, who felt cruelly deceived by her Sweet Robin. Posing as a lonely widower, whose happiness was bound up with her own, he had been counselling her in the strongest terms against marrying Alençon, while he himself was in fact a married man again. She ordered him to the Tower but listened, when her anger had passed, to Sussex who, though he hated Leicester more than any man, persuaded her that so ruthless an act would harm her dignity. He was lodged instead in an isolated building in Greenwich Park 'to take physic', but after a week was allowed to return to his manor at Wanstead, provided he kept away from court until further orders. Mercifully the Queen was preoccupied with the arrival of 'her Frog', who came to Greenwich on 17 August.

She need not have worried about his height or his face, ugly though some may have thought him, even without his pockmarks, as she at once found him sexually attractive and was quite taken by the tilt of his nose. This was more than mere romantic dalliance, for her vanity was appeased; ever since her accession princes had sent messages, presents and deputations, but here was a prince of a great house come to plead his passionate cause himself. 'A frog he would a-wooing go' – and the youth made the middle-aged Queen feel almost a girl again. Alençon did not worry overmuch that she towered over him, and mercifully her French was superb, making what might have been a disastrous first meeting of a bizarre couple, thrown together by circumstance, turn into an idyll. For twelve days as her *incognito* guest, he put in practice Simier's advice, and when he left he was certain he had won her heart. From Boulogne he sent 'a little flower of gold with a frog thereon, and therein Monsieur, his physiognomy'. The omens were indeed propitious.

Leaving aside her attitude to the religious problem, and to the change in constitutional role which marriage would involve

126

for her, how serious were Elizabeth's intentions in 1579? At forty-six she was exactly twice Alençon's age, and dangerously near the menopause. This would account for her emotional instability which marked the active stages of her courtship with Alençon, when she veered from wanting to marry him straightway to losing all interest in him; one day she desperately wanted to have a baby, the next she was dreading the thought of consummation and the dangers of childbirth. At any time Leicester's remarriage would have come as a severe shock, but hearing about it at this crucial stage in her life savaged her affections. The fact that he had left her side for Lettice Knollys threw her into Alençon's arms, for the Frenchman offered her a final chance of fulfilment as a woman, and she knew this was so.

Burghley did not doubt her ability to bear a child, for he had secretly consulted the best medical opinion as well as the views of her ladies. Women over forty-six with a far less suitable physique had produced healthy infants without impairing their constitutions and he was assured that sexual relations and childbearing would improve the Queen's general health. Leicester, Walsingham and Sussex shared his view that the idea that Elizabeth was barren sprang from idle gossip. Clearly, she knew quite as well as Burghley that her doctors were confident about her chances of motherhood and because she was sure a marriage with Alençon would be fruitful, she wanted it to take place. Yet unlike the milkmaid she was not a free agent and would not make so momentous a decision while her subjects were hotly divided on the topic. In the early 'sixties she had found Leicester too controversial a figure to have as her consort and now, in the late 'seventies, she found 'her Frog' had aroused Englishmen's worst prejudices.

There was the legacy of St Bartholomew's Day, which the Puritan John Stubbs exploited in a formidable tract against the French match. Alençon was, he said, the old serpent himself, 'come to seduce the English Eve and to ruin the English paradise', and his manner of courting had been deplorable, visiting Elizabeth *incognito* – 'an unmanlike, unprince-like, French kind of wooing'. Much worse, under the pretext of his private chapel, the Roman mass would return and silence God's word. Preachers developed the theme and the campaign became so virulent that a proclamation forbade further sermons on the

'An unmanlike, unprince-like French kind of wooing'

127

subject. Stubbs was sent for trial accused of sedition with his *Gaping Gulf* and was sentenced to lose his right hand. When the amputation was carried out, he took off his hat with his left hand, cried a brave 'God Save the Queen' before he fainted, and was carried to the Tower. The publisher of the tract lifted up his bleeding arm to tell the crowd: 'I left there a true Englishman's hand.'

Always sensitive to public opinion, Elizabeth was indecisive on the issue she had always insisted was her matter alone and turned to her Council. If they supported her, as she expected – and they had been urging her to marry for twenty years – she would go through with it and make them share the responsibility. Leicester and Hatton with their deep personal feelings would oppose the marriage, yet she expected Burghley to carry the day with a strong vote favouring it. Twelve Councillors sat in secret session for eleven hours and at the end of the exhausting discussion Burghley found he was outnumbered, though he persuaded his colleagues to give an open verdict, and went with Leicester to tell the Queen that until they knew her own views they could make no recommendation. This provoked tears and accusations of insulting her. Later that night she summoned them again to tell them they had a clear duty to urge her to marry, so the full Council passed a unanimous recommendation assenting to her match with Alençon 'if so it shall please her'. Such was scant encouragement, she told them, and if they could not improve on the way they gave advice it was certainly not worth consulting them. Next month when terms were being discussed again with Simier, she insisted on delaying any announcement until she had won general support for the marriage. By then, indeed, she had concluded it was impossible, though she would act out the drama to the end, playing a role that still had an immense appeal for her.

Alençon was becoming more necessary than ever. Relations with Spain were being strained to breaking-point through Drake's privateering in the New World, and Elizabeth did not underestimate Spanish power; the Spanish victory of Lepanto over the Turks was regarded as the most decisive naval action of modern times and now, in 1580, the Duke of Alva had conquered Portugal for Philip II in a matter of weeks. At any time Philip could turn his attention to England and, in a grand

ABOVE Sir Francis Drake, whose privateering raids upon the Spanish Main in the 1570s produced rich prizes for Elizabeth.

128

DI VINO

SIC PARVIS MAGNA

enterprise, honour his pledge to the Pope to rescue Mary and depose Elizabeth. Elizabeth planned to transform the French treaty of 1572 into a full-scale offensive and defensive alliance against Spain and to achieve this she would continue to encourage Alençon to think she would have him. 'If I do not marry him I do not know whether he will remain friendly with me; and if I do I shall not be able to govern the country with the freedom and security I have hitherto enjoyed.' Burghley advised her to marry Alençon only if she wished to and the terms were right, but if she were now lukewarm about him she must deceive him no longer. 'That', she answered, 'is not the opinion of the rest of the Council, but that I should keep him in correspondence.' Such, indeed, was the policy she would follow as long as she dared, to play for time not against matrimony, but against Spain.

When Sir Francis Drake returned from his great voyage round the world in the *Golden Hind*, giving Elizabeth and his other backers a return of 4,700 per cent on their investment with the booty he had taken from Spanish ships and settlements in the New World, she decided to knight him at Deptford. As he knelt before her on the quarterdeck of the *Golden Hind* she joked that she had a golden sword to strike off his head for being a pirate, and then handed the sword to Alençon's new agent, De Marchaumont, to give him the accolade, an unprecedented privilege. As she had climbed aboard one of her garters slipped off and De Marchaumont claimed it as his lawful prize for sending to the Duke. The Queen told him to return it as she had nothing else to keep up her stocking, but promised to surrender it to him on returning to Greenwich, and so the garter joined the nightcap and the other trophies Simier had purloined. Mendoza, the Spanish ambassador, shamed by Drake's knighthood, thought the marriage with Alençon as good as concluded. No expense was spared in entertaining the French commissioners who came over a fortnight later to arrange the long projected treaty, when the highlight of the festivities was a triumph in the tiltyard. Here was enacted an elaborate allegory on the courtship, in which Desire attacked the 'Fortress of Perfect Beauty', though at the end of the day Virtue proved too strong for Desire and the impregnable Fortress was 'to be reserved for the eye of the whole world'. The two-month special embassy, punctuated

OVERLEAF A map of the world in 1581, drawn to commemorate Drake's voyage around the world from December 1577 to September 1580. On his return, Drake was knighted by Elizabeth on board the *Golden Hind* (shown at the bottom of the map) at Deptford.

VERA TOTIVS EXP

Portus Novæ Albionis

ASIA
AMERI:
INDIA ORIENTALIS
NOVA ALBION
TERRA AVSTRALIS
NOVA GUINEA
MAR DI
INDIA
MARE PACIF.
AEQVINOCTIALI
MAR DEL
TROPICVS CANCRI
TROPICVS CAPRICORNI
CIRCVLVS ANTARCTICV

by banquets and *fêtes galantes*, proclaimed the strength of the new *entente* between England and France which would be little weakened if the negotiations with Alençon foundered.

Once the Duke had received further funds from England to pay his troops, who had forced Parma to raise the siege of Cambrai, he embarked on a second visit to Elizabeth; he was, she said, 'the most deserving and constant of all her lovers'. Her Accession Day was celebrated with even greater ceremony than usual and in the evening in the gallery at Whitehall, she told the French ambassador he could inform his King that she and Alençon would definitely marry, and then, turning to her suitor, she kissed him warmly and presented him with a ring from her own finger as a pledge. Londoners reckoned the marriage was 'as good as accomplished' and so did such informed and perceptive men as Burghley and Leicester. That very evening, so the tale is told, the Queen's women, put up to it by Leicester and Hatton, 'wailed and by laying terrors before her' frightened her from marrying. It is certainly true that the next morning she sent for Alençon and told him that after a sleepless night, when her heart warred against her head, she had decided to sacrifice her own happiness for her people's welfare and so could not marry him at present, though her boundless affection for him remained; she might change her mind later, but now she was overwrought. Though she used the warnings of her ladies on the perils of childbearing as an excuse for jilting him, her mind had been quite made up eighteen months earlier, when she learnt the extent of her Council's opposition. Since then she had been acting her part superbly.

The Duke acted out his part with dignity. Instead of rushing back to the Netherlands in a huff, he stayed on at court hopefully, enjoying his banquets for another three months, unaware that he had outstayed his welcome. In the end it came down to haggling. Leicester thought he might be bribed to leave England with £200,000, but the Queen was horrified at the thought of spending so much on him, so he was given £10,000 in cash with a promise of £50,000 more when he had put to sea. Elizabeth accompanied him as far as Canterbury in February 1582 and wept as they parted. She braved her melancholy by writing a poem *On Monsieur's Departure*:

I grieve, yet dare not show my discontent;
   I love, and yet am forced to seem to hate;
I dote, but dare not what I meant;
   I seem stark mute, yet inwardly do prate.
I am, and am not – freeze, and yet I burn,
Since from myself my other self I turn.

Fondly she wrote to the Duke saying she would give a million pounds to see her Frog swimming again in the Thames; he was the man she had so nearly married. After the Council's opposition in 1579, which fairly reflected opinion in the country, she knew marriage with him was out of the question. She kept up the pretence but she knew that because of the passing years this would be her last courtship. Elizabeth concluded that it was better to remain a virgin Queen than become a childless wife to an unpopular foreign prince. When Alençon died of a fever in the battlefield against Parma thirty months later, she put her court in mourning out of respect for his memory, but in fact even as she was writing her verses modelled on Petrarch, lamenting becoming an old maid, she had fallen under the spell of Walter Raleigh, a West Countryman twenty years her junior, who was tall, unlike Alençon, poetic and 'damnable proud'.

6 The Court of Elizabeth 1558-1603

T HE COURT, implicit in a personal monarchy, was the setting in which the Queen lived out her public and private lives, so that attendance on her became the social obligation of the aristocracy and the goal of lesser mortals. This was the centre of affairs, the fount of patronage and power, the regular avenue to profit and promotion, so it exercised a magnetic attraction that was irresistible. Her great household resembled a large family, under a matriarch who expected her 'relations' to be about her, justifying their aristocratic privilege by service to her. For the courtier proper to be away from her side was to be in the shadows, forgotten, deprived of news and even of informed gossip. 'It is a world to be here, to see the humours of the time', wrote one basking in the sunshine of high favour, but well knowing that the clouds could gather without warning. 'Blessed are they that can be away and live contented.' Like any family the court had its feuds, when temperaments clashed, and its favourite sons had their nicknames; Burghley she called her 'Spirit', while Leicester's 'Eyes' symbolised her own omni-presence and Hatton's 'Lids' represented her own understanding in turning a blind eye – a playful way of underlining her motto *video et taceo*, 'I see but keep silent'. Elizabeth sought by domi-nating her court to maintain a judicious balance between rival factions so that peace was kept.

This was essentially a society of Councillors, peers and senior officials. Though as servants of the Crown they were entitled to board and lodging at court, their wives could not expect to share this privilege as of right and relatively few women held posts in the Queen's Chamber. In theory anyone who could boast the status of gentleman had access to the court, but in practice one needed a patron, for, as Lord Burghley put it, a man without a friend at court was like a hop without a pole. Happy the youth whose figure stood out in the crowd to provoke interest or recognition as the Queen passed by. The seventeen-year-old Welsh lad who later became Lord Herbert of Cherbury enjoyed the kind of début that hundreds dreamt about, when he came to court more from curiosity than ambition. Much later he recalled the scene.

As it was the manner of the times for all men to kneel down before the great Queen Elizabeth, I was likewise upon my knees in the Presence Chamber when she passed by to the Chapel at

136

Whitehall. As soon as she saw me she stopped and, swearing her usual oath, demanded 'Who is this?' Everybody there present looked upon me, until Sir James Croft, a pensioner, finding the Queen stayed, returned back and told who I was ...

To be noticed and talked to was very heaven. Some invested a fortune with tailors to be turned out as court dandies that they might perchance catch Her Majesty's eye as a means of setting a foot on the lowest rung of the ladder of preferment; others less ambitious for themselves wanted no more than 'to have the twinkling of one beam of the splendiferous planet'.

There was much discussion about the best way of training youth for the Queen's service, and men recognised that the two branches of education followed in earlier times – of the clerk in school and university, and of the knight at arms graduating from a great household to win his spurs for chivalry in warfare – needed bringing together. The courtier of the later sixteenth century in England, as on the Continent, was expected to be something of a clerk *and* something of a knight, a rounded person in the Renaissance mould no less versatile in his parts than the mistress he served. In the literature of the day he was not merely a wise councillor framing policies or a skilled warrior making strategic decisions from his tent or flagship, but a companion excelling in wit and fashion in whom his sovereign was well pleased. The standard manual of courtesy was the Italian Castiglione's *Book of the Courtier* which Burghley's brother-in-law, Sir Thomas Hoby, had translated; it enjoyed a considerable vogue and for the rest of the reign a copy of it would be found on the shelves of country gentlemen with few pretensions to learning, next to Tusser's *Five Hundred Points of Good Husbandry*, Foxe's *Book of Martyrs* and the Bible. Here they read that the perfect courtier must aim at all-round ability, being skilled in languages, well prepared to converse know-ledgeably with his sovereign on art and poetry, to play at least one instrument well and sing a part in tune, and to be an accomplished dancer, horseman and tennis player. Under this new code of 'courtesy' a man developed his personality as he served his royal mistress. Since court was a highly competitive society, in Castiglione's words he must endeavour 'to surpass others somewhat in everything' and yet take care to achieve this success by a somewhat effortless superiority.

> *'To have the twinkling of one beam of the splendiferous planet'*

The vogue for Italian manners which Hoby's translation introduced, led to the popularity of the grand tour of Italy, and young Englishmen hoped their travels in such civilised cities would provide a passport to Elizabeth's court when they returned home. After the papal bull deposing Elizabeth, however, some rubbed in the dangers of a sojourn in the states of the Counter-Reformation; 'Suffer not thy sons to pass the Alps', counselled Burghley who believed with the homespun Roger Ascham that one year's study at home would do a young gentleman more good than three spent in Italy, for any who stayed in 'Circe's court' became changed into 'an Italianate Englishman, who is the devil incarnate'. For all his scholarship, blunt Yorkshire Ascham lacked the courtier's graces, and despite his attacks the grand tour retained its popularity until with the outbreak of the war with Spain, service afloat or in the field in the Netherlands or France provided more exciting ways of completing one's education for court.

Elizabeth valued intelligence in a man no less than she appreciated an ability to sing songs to the lute, write lyric poetry or excel in the tiltyard. Gentle compliments from a man of wit were on quite a different plane from the empty flattery of a dullard. She might have defined a courtier as one whose manners and conversation no less than his judgment and sense of responsibility entirely satisfied her. Those who broke the strict rules of etiquette on formal occasions were left in no doubt of their effrontery; a young buck 'being more bold than well-mannered' at a palace reception in 1582 stood on the carpet of the cloth of estate and 'did almost lean upon the cushions' where the Queen was sitting, and she reprimanded her Lord Chamberlain for allowing such behaviour. But a man who had the intuition to respond to her when she wanted distraction from

Italian stringed instrument called a 'cetera', made in stained and carved maplewood, 1582.

the cares of state, abandon formality and treat her as a woman stood a strong chance of gaining her favour as a Queen; if he could convey that he was also a little in love with her and play the masquerade in the way she wanted, then he would certainly feel he was treading on air.

As her father's daughter Elizabeth wanted her court to become a great cultural centre, an academy where illustrious men found fellowship and patronage, but she was not prepared to spend nearly as freely as King Henry. John Lyly whose *Euphues, or the Anatomy of Wit*, the earliest English novel, had won him golden opinions at an early age, hoped to achieve the post of Master of the Revels. To fit himself for the task of producing dramatic performances and masques he deserted romance for writing a series of 'court comedies', as he termed them, and then in 1585 embarked on *Endymion*, an allegorical play on the subject of Leicester's passions. The Earl was the shepherd Endymion, who adored his heavenly mistress Cynthia, the Moon (the Queen), but was entangled in earthly loves for Tellus (Douglas Sheffield) and Floscula (Lettice Knollys). The play was popular at court, but if tackling so risqué a theme did Lyly no harm, it did nothing to forward his claims to royal patronage. Waiting for dead men's shoes was a dispiriting business and he begged for present aid. 'Thirteen years Your Highness' servant, but yet nothing', he wrote. 'Twenty friends that though they say they will be sure, I find them sure to be slow. A thousand hopes, but all nothing; a hundred promises, but yet nothing. Thus, casting up the inventory of my friends, hopes, promises and times the *summa totalis* amounteth to just nothing.' Alas, Lyly died before the reigning Master of the Revels.

Edmund Spenser, hungering for patronage, became no less disillusioned. The 'April' Eclogue in his *Shepheards Calendar* was a paean of praise for the Queen, but all he got out of it was banishment to Ireland, as secretary to the Lord Deputy, and throughout his sojourn there he never ceased to hope for a place at Cynthia's court. In 1589 he came over to England to present to her the first three books of the *Faerie Queene*, which bore a royal dedication, and though Elizabeth later awarded him a pension of £50 a year, there was no post in her train for the laureate of her court who had written the greatest poem since

Music by William Byrd
for the Twelfth Night
festivities of 1590 at Sir
John Petre's home at
Ingatestone, Essex. Byrd
was fetched down from
the Chapel Royal in
London for Christmastide.

Chaucer. One aim of this elaborate allegory was 'to fashion a
gentleman or noble person in virtuous and gentle discipline'; a
secondary aim was the glorification of his sovereign in her two
personalities as Queen and as 'a most virtuous and beautiful
lady', so that Fairyland became located in Elizabethan England,
peopled with characters who were readily identified, with
Elizabeth herself appearing in the different roles of the virgin
huntress, the chaste Britomart and Gloriana the Fairy Queen.
Spenser's superb command of language enabled him to dazzle
the reader with the brilliance of his poetic gifts, just as Gloriana
dazzled her court; yet he felt sadly let down, and in *Mother
Hubberds Tale* satirised the life of the court, dwelling on the
miseries of suitors:

140

To lose good days that better might be spent;
To waste long nights in pensive discontent;
To spend today, to be put back tomorrow;
To feed on hope, to pine with fear and sorrow;
To have thy Prince's grace, yet want her Peers;
To have thy asking, yet wait many years ...

Fretting and fawning, waiting as money and hope ebbed away, Spenser found the indignity of the system unbearable. No man, he said, should be tempted to leave a humble home to seek his fortune at court, for all was but a vain shadow.

Musicians fared much better. Thomas Tallis and William Byrd, successively Masters of the Music of the Chapel Royal, were jointly granted the monopoly of publishing music of all kinds, even of ruled 'manuscript' paper. Tallis, once organist of Waltham Abbey, had spent forty-three years in the royal service, spanning every stage of the English Reformation, with a wonderful range of compositions. Byrd, whose heart remained in the old Latin mass, continued the great traditions set in King Henry's Chapel Royal and was never in danger of being prosecuted for recusancy, for Elizabeth could find no fault in him as a musician. Christopher Tye, who had taught her the virginals, was appointed rector of Doddington, Cambridgeshire, the wealthiest living in England, with permission to absent himself from his parish for long periods so he could be at court. It was the same with the sixty or so instrumentalists who

Thomas Tallis (left) and William Byrd (right), successively Masters of Music of the Chapel Royal under Elizabeth. Tallis had begun his service under Henry VIII and both musicians continued the great traditions set in Henry's Chapel Royal.

formed 'the Queen's Musick', for their talents were rewarded ungrudgingly.

Gifts in cash or kind to officials of the household had long been a feature of promoting suits, from a coin in the palm of a door-keeper to a length of silk to the Lord Chamberlain, and the value of such perquisites of office far exceeded the stipends at every level. The Queen, too, shared in this regular present giving and at one time suitors were expected to send in their gifts to her before they could obtain an audience. All at court were expected to exchange presents with Her Majesty on New Year's Day. Invariably she gave gilt plate, the weight depending on the seniority of the individual, so that while Leicester received one hundred ounces, Smyth the dustman was given twenty and a maid of honour ten. Elizabeth had drawn up what amounted to a balance sheet of these gifts, though the value of the presents to her was omitted unless it was money. Here again the person's rank dictated how much he would have to spend. The dustman could quite reasonably offer a roll of cambric, but the people closest to her knew they must produce something costly; it was only a scholar who could get away with something from his pen instead of his purse, and Roger Ascham was to die from a chill caught sitting up all night to finish his annual poem – a grim warning to others. On New Year's Day 1587 Leicester offered a magnificently jewelled purse and a brooch; his stepson, Essex, a 'fair jewel of gold like a rainbow'; and Heneage, now Treasurer of the Household, a gold pomander and chain set with pearls. That year Hatton's gifts were easily the most lavish – a coronet and an ornamented collar of gold, sparkling with diamonds, with enamelled links and jewelled pendants, and also a set of fifteen gold buttons set with seed pearls, each carrying a Latin tag that praised the Queen's glory. There was nothing from the Earl of Oxford and the jewels sent by his Countess were noted in the list as 'very mean', though she was in financial difficulties. Of the others, Blanche Parry of the Privy Chamber gave an ornament of rubies and gold in the form of a serpent's tongue, while Drake had brought the kind of expensive novelty that absolutely delighted her – a jewelled fan that showed the Queen's portrait when opened. Lavish presents meant a great deal to her and as the years went by she became really avaricious, so that in her last days it was noted

Gold enamelled pendant in a boat shape, probably of Venetian work.

142

that everyone at court was required to make her offerings not only at the New Year but on her Accession Day and birthday as well, 'and when they cannot give anything, she gladly takes a dozen angels'.

Despite the rich pickings from patronage the costs of maintaining oneself and one's servants at court to keep up appearances could be crippling. The average courtier was forced to live well above his means and some were heavily in debt. No one was surprised that when Leicester died he owed the Queen £34,000 and when Hatton died the sum was rather more. It was because Essex's disastrous finances could not bear the non-renewal of the profitable wine duties that he stumbled into rebellion and most of the peers who came out with him were bankrupt too. Perhaps the cautious Lord North came off as well as anybody, for he considered it was worth losing £40 a month to Elizabeth at cards – for she hated not winning – to stay in favour.

Like her forefathers Elizabeth made a regular round of her palaces and country houses, moving principally between Richmond, Hampton Court, Whitehall, Greenwich, Eltham and Windsor, with less frequent stays at Oatlands, near Weybridge, Hatfield, Hunsdon and Woodstock. Removals involved considerable organisation, for the court in all its aspects moved with the Queen, making up a great entourage of officials, guards and servants, with a hundred and more carts conveying supplies and even furniture; Elizabeth certainly stayed as guest in a number of houses still standing, but she

Richmond Palace from a drawing by Anthony van Wyngaerde. The palace was built by Elizabeth's grandfather, Henry VII, on the site of the ancient palace of Sheen, and was named after his earldom in Yorkshire. It was to be one of Elizabeth's favourite residences.

143

always slept in her own bed, brought by the groom of the wardrobe of beds. At a whim she would sometimes cancel her departure, decide on a sudden removal to another royal residence or change her itinerary, so that carefully laid plans were overturned. A carter, waiting in the courtyard for the order to drive away, greeted news of the third change of plans in a day with the fruity comment that clearly 'the Queen is a woman as well as my wife', but Elizabeth had heard him and throwing down some coins from the gallery called him a villain!

The Queen made much of her summer progresses when she journeyed further afield than the Home Counties. Earlier sovereigns had visited different parts of their realm for specific reasons – like her father's state visit to York in 1541 – or had enjoyed prolonged hunting expeditions, but Elizabeth was the

The Great Bed of Ware, a massive piece of Elizabethan furniture carved and inlaid with oak. This was the type of bed in which Elizabeth slept, and which had to move around with her on her journeys.

A late sixteenth-century 'Nonsuch' chest richly inlaid with light-coloured woods. It derives its name from the architectural scenes in perspective, which are reminiscent of the Tudor palace of Nonsuch.

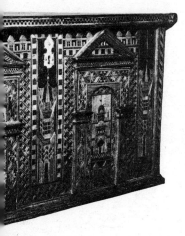

first to take a regular summer holiday away from London, getting to know different parts of the country and showing herself to her people there. For nine-tenths of the year greater London had the Queen to itself, but in the summer progress it was the turn of provincial England to pay homage as she passed by, offering loyal addresses and fat purses, staring and cheering. For many country folk the chance of seeing her more than once in a lifetime was remote. She responded to their welcomes by countless friendly gestures. Passing through Huntingdonshire a rustic fellow ran up to the royal coachman and breathlessly asked him to stop, 'that I may speak to the Queen', and though the incident made her laugh, she gave him her hand to kiss so that he would reckon himself the proudest man in England. At Warwick the recorder had been trembling with nervousness at having to make a speech, but after his ordeal was over she told him: 'You were not so afraid of me as I was of you.' It was not an English annalist but a Spanish ambassador that noted her popularity when Elizabeth visited Berkshire:

> She was received everywhere with great acclamation and signs of joy, as is customary in this country, whereat she was exceedingly pleased and told me so, giving me to understand how beloved she was by her subjects and how highly she esteemed this …. She would order her carriage sometimes to be taken where the crowd seemed thickest and stood up and thanked her people.

Prolonged travel on poor roads was arduous and often the itinerant court averaged only three miles an hour. When the Queen at last reached Bristol in 1574, well behind schedule after heavy storms, she composed a prayer of thanksgiving 'for preserving me in this long and dangerous journey'. Next year she had an even longer period away from London, visiting Worcester, staying for three weeks of a hot July with Leicester at Kenilworth, where he had staged such varied entertainments for her delight as a firework display, a production of the Coventry Hock Tuesday play and a water pageant on the theme of the Delivery of the Lady of the Lake, until she moved on to visit Lady Essex at Chartley, near Stafford. This was the furthest north the Queen ever reached, though she had hoped that year to carry on to Shrewsbury and in to North Wales; she always wanted to visit York, as her father had done, but plans had to be abandoned. Among her notable progresses were those to

Southampton, Oxford and Cambridge early in the reign and a prolonged stay in East Anglia in 1578, when on leaving the second city of the kingdom she brought tears to people's eyes by saying 'I have laid up in my head such goodwill, as I shall never forget Norwich', and they knew they would never see her in those parts again. The borough of Leicester was always out of luck; in four different years she was expected to come and elaborate plans were made for welcoming her, but on each occasion the visit was cancelled. Though in the last twenty years of the reign distant progresses were no longer staged, more on account of the international situation than the Queen's age, she still took to the roads each summer, riding side-saddle or in a litter, to visit the Home Counties.

On these progresses Elizabeth expected to be entertained by her chief courtiers who, after all, lived at her expense for so much of the year in their grace and favour lodgings at Whitehall and the other palaces. While the itinerary was being drafted, all those in danger of having to play host in their country mansions began to make excuses – the house was too small, time was too short to make adequate preparations, the roads in those parts were unfit for the Queen's carriage; most were too proud to plead they could not afford the luxury of a royal visit. Once it was clear that the Queen was not going to be put off, it was important to try to persuade her to make her visit short. The Earl of Bedford desperately hoped her 'tarrying be not above two nights and a day' at Woburn. This cheeseparing attitude was quite illogical, because the aristocracy as a whole were indulging in an extravagant building spree from 1570 onwards, erecting 'prodigy houses' or outsize country seats specially designed for entertaining their sovereign on progress, with the plans of the rooms modelled on the domestic arrangements at the palace. Burghley exceeded his purse in building Theobalds in Hertfordshire to make it fit for the Queen, but then complained that each visit she paid to the house that delighted her cost him about £3,000. There was always a wonderfully warm welcome when the Queen visited the Norrises at Rycote, where Elizabeth had stayed with old Lord Williams of Thame the night before her imprisonment at Woodstock. Lady Norris, whom she affectionately called her 'Crow', was exceedingly angry with Leicester for trying to

In 1564, William Cecil bought the manor of Theobalds, near Enfield, and began to build his magnificent new house there. This drawing by John Thorpe probably shows the courtyard elevation of the house, which has since been demolished. Elizabeth loved to stay with Cecil at Theobalds, and a special suite was set aside for her visits.

persuade her against staying in the house. Though certain charges for food and drink might be recovered from the Treasurer of the household, the host's charge for entertaining the whole itinerant court was staggering, so friends, neighbours and dependants were expected to rally round with gifts. Lord Keeper Egerton skilfully extracted many presents for his larder and cellar at Harefield in 1602, including a pipe of claret and some sturgeon from the Lord Mayor of London and seventy-nine sides of venison from fellow peers.

Progresses were unpopular with many courtiers, who with the end of term longed to be off to their own homes instead of fitting uneasily into other peoples'. The principal suite in any 'prodigy house' became the Queen's quarters, but the assignment of chambers to others was a ticklish matter. There were frequent complaints from men used to comfortable rooms in Whitehall who were having to put up with mean accommodation. On the royal visit to Archbishop Whitgift's palace at Croydon, Raleigh installed himself in the lodgings set aside for Hatton, provoking a dreadful scene in which the Queen lost her temper with the Lord Chamberlain, Lord Howard of

Sir Henry Lee, Elizabeth's Champion at the Tilt, by Antonio Mor. He issued a challenge to run a tilt against all-comers annually on the Queen's Accession Day, 17 November. From this vow arose a series of tournaments which reached spectacular proportions by the 1580s. To these festivals, knights came in elaborate fancy dress surrounded by actors and musicians who acted out dramas in the tiltyard. In 1592, Lee entertained Elizabeth at a great tournament at Ditchley, commemorated by the Ditchley portrait (*see* frontispiece).

Effingham, for allowing Hatton to be snubbed. Men in the lowlier ranks had to make do with outhouses, inns and tents. Sir Harry Lee refused to put up with a tent in Hampshire and left the court: 'I am old and come now evil away with the inconveniences of progress', he wrote.

Besides banquets, the host had to provide suitable entertainment and was expected to make a present to the Queen as she was leaving. There would be madrigals sung from the long gallery, pageants in the gardens (weather permitting) and plays in the hall. The host, eager to impress, would attempt to stage a novel spectacle of the kind that delighted Her Majesty and hope that those prolific, popular court poets, William Churchyard and George Gascoigne, would complete suitable verses in time for the visit. When Elizabeth came to Hertford's house at Elvetham she found a great pond had been dug in the shape of a half-moon, with three islands on which stood buildings representing in turn a fort, a ship and a snail, as the setting for a notable 'triumph' in which she would be praised in a rich vein of allegory. Lord Egerton excelled himself in the welcome he devised for her at Harefield. Inside the park gates a rustic bailiff and a dairymaid spoke their bantering dialogue, ending when the latter gave Elizabeth a jewelled fork and rake, but on the steps of the house she sat down in a chair to listen to the discussion between 'Time', dressed as an hour glass, and 'Place', in a robe like a brick house, on the honour of entertaining their royal visitor – the Sun Queen. 'But say, poor Place' (asked 'Time') 'in which manner did'st thou entertain the sun?' 'I received his glory and was filled with it', came the happy response. These characters reappeared as she ended her stay, but now dressed in mourning, to give her a jewelled anchor, since 'this harbour is too little for you and you will hoist sail and be gone'. The gifts Egerton's predecessor, Lord Keeper Puckering, presented when Elizabeth left his house at Kew included a fan with the handle encrusted with diamonds, a jewelled nosegay worth £400, a pair of virginals and some clothes. The criterion of a successful visit was how long she would stay, and if Sir William Clarke saved his money he lost all credit at court when Elizabeth came to his mansion at Burnham and quickly moved on, for his frugal arrangements 'pleased nobody, but gave occasion to have his miserliness and vanity spread far and wide'.

148

The court would then return to Whitehall or Greenwich, which had been thoroughly cleaned in the Queen's absence, as autumn set in and with it the fear of the plague was forgotten until the next summer. It was here, on her home ground, that the Queen chose to receive ambassadors and Parliamentary deputations, as always commanding the stage and placing her troublesome petitioners at a psychological disadvantage. When commissioners from Flanders had come to England in 1582 to hasten Alençon's return to the battlefield – which was just what Elizabeth herself wanted – she rated them for their churlish behaviour towards him: 'You shoemakers, carpenters and heretics, how dare you speak in such terms to a man of royal blood like the Duke of Alençon. I would have you know that when you approach him, or me, you are in the presence of the two greatest princes in Christendom.' When a Polish ambassador came in 1597 to deliver a long Latin harangue to her on the iniquities of English seamen in searching neutral ships and to threaten his master's displeasure, Elizabeth 'made one of the best answers *extempore* in Latin that I ever heard', noted Robert

In 1591 Elizabeth visited the Earl of Hertford at Elvetham in Hampshire. Hertford had dug a special half-moon-shaped pond with three islands, on which were placed a fort, a ship and a snail. With these, a complex allegorical 'triumph' was performed before the Queen.

Cecil. 'Was this the business that your king has sent you about?' she thundered. 'Surely I can hardly believe that if the king himself were present he would have used such language.' The man was finally put in his place and dismissed to confer with the Council, for he had shown himself to be a mere herald not an ambassador – even of an elected king. Right at the end of the reign, when the Venetian Scaramelli was given an audience to present his credentials, the Queen was just as forceful in Italian invective. Why had the Venetian Republic waited until she had reigned for forty-five years, she asked, before it honoured her with a diplomatic representative? 'Never has it given a sign of holding me or my kingdom in that esteem which other princes and other potentates have not refused. Nor can I assume that my sex has brought me this demerit, for my sex cannot diminish my prestige ...' And yet Venice was in a different category from Poland, so she relented a little and with a smile asked him about her Italian; had she spoken it well? 'for I learnt it when a child and believe I have not forgotten it'. Scaramelli had certainly been overawed in the Presence Chamber by the imposing figure in silver and white taffeta, trimmed with gold, blazing with jewels on her head, neck, wrists and dress, with 'great pearls like pears' and an enormous ruff, dominating the scene.

The life of the court was closely interwoven with the life of the capital, or rather of the twin cities of London and West-minster, and great houses for Arundel, Burghley, Leicester and other peers led from the Strand, the link between the two. A main road passed through Whitehall Palace and there was a further right of way from the public landing-stage through the courtyards. Anyone could come into the grounds to see the Queen go in procession to the Chapel Royal, any who queued early enough, could watch bear-baiting in the tiltyard, cock-fighting or royal tennis. The Accession Day tournament in the tiltyard, the only organised form of sport of the age, attracted thousands of spectators, many of them paying 12d. for a seat in one of the stands not so far from Her Majesty, to cheer Oxford, Blount, Essex and the other seeded champions breaking a lance for the honour of their sovereign lady and the prize of a jewel the victor would receive at the end of the day from her own beautiful hands. At state banquets and masques there were

The picture here set down
within this letter .T.
Aright doth shew the forme
of Tharlton vnto the, shap

When hee in pleasaunt wise
the Counterfet expreste
of Clowne wth cote of russet
and sturtups wth y[e] reste, hew.

Whoe merry many made
when he appeard in sight
The graue and wise as well as
at him did take delight, rud.

The partie nowe is gone,
and closlie clad in claye,
Of all the Iesters in the land,
he bare the praise awaie.

Now hath he plaid his pte
and sure he is of this,
If he in Christe did die to liue
with him in lasting blis.

Richard Tarleton, Elizabeth's favourite clown. He had acted in Leicester's company and was the most outstanding of the troupe of players known as the Queen's Men, founded in 1583 for entertainment at court. Perhaps he was Shakespeare's 'Yorick' as well as Spenser's 'Pleasant Willy'.

The Elizabethan Theatre

Elizabeth was a great patron of the theatre and defended her actors from the attacks of the Puritans. Her own company of actors was created in 1583, and was quickly followed by those of Lord Howard of Effingham and Lord Hunsdon. For these companies, new theatres were built on the south bank in London and playwrights were inspired to write new works.

LEFT Richard Burbage who was the most popular actor of his day. He built the Globe Theatre and produced most of Shakespeare's plays there.
RIGHT Ben Jonson, actor and dramatist. The first reference to his plays comes in Philip Henslowe's account of 1597. In 1598, he produced his comedy *Every Man in his Humour* at the Curtain Theatre – Shakespeare was one of the performers.

LEFT The Swan Theatre from a pen and ink drawing made by Jan de Witte in 1596.

RIGHT Edward Alleyn, one of the directors of Lord Howard's company and a leading Elizabethan actor.
FAR RIGHT William Shakespeare – the most celebrated dramatist of the Elizabethan age – from an engraving by Martin Droeshout.

To the Reader.

This *Figure*, that thou here feeft put,
    It was for gentle *Shakefpeare* cut;
Wherein the *Graver* had a ftrife
    With *Nature*, to out-doe the *Life* :
O, could he but haue drawn his *Wit*
    As well in *Braffe*, as he has hit
His *Face* ; the *Print* would then furpaffe
    All, that was euer writ in *Braffe*.
But fince he cannot, *Reader*, look
    Not on his *Picture*, but his *Book*.

                                B. *J.*

153

generally a number of seats available in a high gallery from which ordinary subjects could eavesdrop on the great of the land enjoying themselves, and already the corridors of Whitehall leading to the great staircase, which gave on to the private apartments, had the air of a national gallery, for the public was admitted free of charge to see the pictures and tapestries on the walls. Like her father Elizabeth considered the staring of the crowds a form of paying homage to her and in term time there was a good chance of seeing her almost every day – a fact that alarmed her Councillors when plots to assassinate her were rife. A schoolboy, Godfrey Goodman, destined for a bishopric, remembered waiting by the Whitehall Gate to catch a glimpse of her by torchlight in the December after the defeat of the Armada, which had given a tremendous fillip to her popularity. As always, a crowd had gathered in the yard and when she left the Council room the spectators cried 'God save Your Majesty', to which Elizabeth made her customary response 'God bless you all my good people'. They all cheered again and she acknowledged this by saying, 'You may well have a greater prince, but you shall never have a more loving prince'. This everyday incident at court made a great impression on the young Goodman and his fellows so that 'all the way home we did nothing but talk what an admirable Queen she was and how we would adventure our lives to do her service'.

'We would adventure our lives to do her service'

A final aspect of court life with far-reaching consequences was the patronage of the drama. Under William Hunnis, their master, the choristers of the Queen's Chapel had been increasingly used for taking women's parts in the interludes of masques and other spectacles. This aroused the especial wrath of the Puritans who, as self-appointed censors, declared that 'plays will never be suppressed while Her Majesty's unfledged minions flaunt it in silks and satins'. At the same time the various dramatic companies supported by the Earls of Leicester, Sussex and Oxford were under heavy fire for their productions and the Puritan City Fathers aimed at closing every theatre in London. The Queen's active support saved Elizabethan drama from being sacrificed for narrow religious principles; she intervened to prevent the chilling winds of the Reformation blowing away the Renaissance from England and in 1583 she formed her own dramatic company, 'Queen Elizabeth's Men',

154

by recruiting a dozen leading actors from the existing troupes, headed by Richard Tarleton, a born comedian who could always make her laugh by his cheeky repartee. Who but Tarleton would have dared to tell the Queen to remove the paint from her face? Queen Elizabeth's men did not confine their performances to the court but toured the provinces and the Queen forced the Lord Mayor of London to lease them a playhouse.

Following her example, Lord Howard of Effingham, the Lord Admiral, formed his own company, engaging Edward Alleyn and Philip Henslowe to direct it, and it was through this company that Christopher Marlowe was given the opportunity of displaying his genius. Soon the Lord Chamberlain's Men were formed and in 1594, when Lord Hunsdon reorganised the company, it became linked with the name of William Shakespeare, who was to give court and capital the greatest series of plays in all history. Elizabeth went with Essex to see the first performance of *A Comedy of Errors* and five months later was guest of honour at the celebrations arranged for the wedding between Lord Derby and Lady Elizabeth Vere, when *A Midsummer's Night's Dream* had its début. In the winter of 1601–2 as many as ten new plays were performed at court; by now Ben Jonson had established himself as a playwright and the Queen delighted in the production of his *Cynthia's Revels* by the children of the Chapel. But for her vigorous defence of the drama the theatres would have been closed, as the Puritans under Cromwell were in fact to close them, and then the world would never have known the contents of the First Folio.

7 The Decisive Years 1584-91

WITH ELIZABETH'S DETERMINATION to remain unmarried the problem of Mary Queen of Scots became even more acute. In the crisis of 1569 Elizabeth had been bold enough to require Huntingdon to have Mary secretly put to death if Norfolk led an army. Three years later, after the Massacre of St Bartholomew, she had offered to surrender Mary to the Regent Mar of Scotland on the understanding that her trial and execution would follow, though the plan came to nothing when the Scots demanded 3,000 English soldiers to maintain order during the Queen's execution, and Elizabeth could not risk her complicity in such a plot being revealed. Thereafter Mary remained a forlorn prisoner, her spirits kept up solely by thoughts of being rescued. Elizabeth, the prisoner of policy, wished she could find a way out of the labyrinth; she could not believe she had been wrong in keeping Mary in custody and to release her now would be to admit not only that her policy had failed but that her grounds for adopting it had been unjustified. In 1581 no more than in 1568 could she allow Mary to travel to the Continent to join the enemies of England and if she were to be set at large at home the position would be even more dangerous, with recusants and new converts rallying to the Jesuit missionaries who had come over from Douai.

In vain did the Jesuits Edmund Campion and Robert Parsons declare that they had returned home to save men's souls, not to be involved with politics, for the bull of 1570 had made all the difference. Evidence of plots to take the Queen's life or of more ambitious schemes for the Catholic powers to invade England and set Mary on Elizabeth's throne provoked an outburst of anti-papalism far more vituperative than in the 1530s, and the seminary priests were regarded as the shock troops of the enterprise. The Vatican had ruled that any person who assassinated 'that guilty woman of England' with the intention of furthering God's cause would have treasure laid up for him in heaven. Parliament had panicked into drafting draconian legislation against the Catholics, which Elizabeth herself had moderated. Even so, erring Englishmen were to be taxed out of their recusancy by being forced to pay £20 a month in addition to the shilling a week fine for not attending Anglican services imposed in 1559. Proclamations called on subjects to stand fast in their allegiance to Queen and Church, 'free from

Edmund Campion, the Jesuit missionary sent over from the college at Douai to make converts to Catholicism, and to contact Catholic families in England. He was executed at Tyburn in 1581 'for conspiring the death of the Queen and to raise sedition'.

PREVIOUS PAGES Lord Howard of Effingham's flagship, *Thr Ark Royal*, at the time of the Spanish Armada in 1588.

A seventeenth-century broad-sheet showing the Catholic plots against Elizabeth from the rebellion of the Northern Earls to the Spanish Armada.

the burden of the Roman tyranny'. Campion was hunted down and great efforts were made to induce him to retract, but he was immovable, only asking that he might take part in a public disputation – a form of 'teach-in' that the Council decided was too risky to stage, though he was allowed a more controlled debate in the Chapel of the Tower with two deans. He was

unable, despite his great learning and vigorous manner, to face the dread political realities. To purvey papal pastoral theology was high treason as the law stood, though Elizabeth insisted Campion be tried by the old treason statute and not, as Burghley wanted, for his religious offence under the Act of 1581, and so he went to Tyburn 'for conspiring the death of the Queen and to raise sedition'.

These were the years of tyrannicide. The unstable John Somerville from Warwickshire planned to shoot the Queen with a pistol and 'see her head set upon a pole'. Then Francis Throckmorton plotted for the Duke de Guise to invade Sussex as a Catholic liberator to set Mary on the throne. If such schemes sound to us fantastic, the danger to Elizabeth seemed very real when, within the year, William the Silent had been assassinated in July 1584. The Queen made light of these perils, alarming

Leicester and others by the few precautions she took for her own safety. While she was returning to Whitehall at the end of 1583, crowds knelt by the road imploring her to take especial care of her person, yet she had little sympathy for their loving concern and refused to alter her routine if it meant cutting herself off from her subjects. How happy Hatton was to be assured that a bout of sickness was not produced by poison but by the novel practice of eating cereals for breakfast – 'a concoction of barley, sodden with sugar and water, all made exceedingly thick with bread', that had upset the Queen's stomach.

The immediate answer to the Catholic Enterprise against England lay not in bodyguards and increased protection but in the remarkable system of counter-espionage devised by Sir Francis Walsingham, who had achieved distinction for the

Mary Queen of Scots in a double portrait with her son, James VI of Scotland, painted in 1583 from imagination by an unknown artist. She had not seen her son since his infancy. Nevertheless, right up to the time of her execution in 1587, she was trying to meet her cousin Elizabeth and to effect a reconciliation with her son.

162

dénouement of the Ridolfi conspiracy. He had been ambassador at Paris at the time of the Massacre of St Bartholomew and in 1573 came into his own as Principal Secretary of State, an arduous post at the heart of domestic and foreign affairs which he held single-handed until his death. Grounded in militant Puritanism from his Cambridge days, his religious fervour increased with the years and, no less than his son-in-law, Sir Philip Sidney, he cast Elizabeth in the role of champion of Protestantism in Europe, to aid French Huguenots and Dutch Calvinists against the House of Guise, Philip of Spain and the Papacy. To intercept a letter, crack a cipher, analyse intelligence reports from agents abroad, eavesdrop on a conversation or extract evidence with the help of the rack were all for Walsingham ways of fighting the good fight against the Church of Rome and of sharpening a sword to slay 'the bosom serpent', Mary. Elizabeth nicknamed him her 'Spy' and 'the papists accused him as a cunning workman in complotting his business'. His spies patiently trailed Throckmorton for six months before they took him into custody from a lodging-house by the docks and, when he stoically revealed nothing from his first racking, Walsingham ordered a second session on the dreadful instrument, correctly predicting that he would break down. Walsingham's *tour de force* was to be the unravelling of the Babington conspiracy.

Mary, a proud, tragic figure, clutched at straws and passed the long hours working at her embroidery, taking pleasure in her pet animals and keeping up a vast correspondence, including a series of letters to Elizabeth in which she complained of her ill usage and the unhealthy conditions of her various residences. She asked still for a meeting with her cousin, if only for two hours, so that the cankered differences between them might be settled before she died and a reconciliation effected with her son, King James. Elizabeth would have been content to keep up the pleasantries by sending Mary presents she knew she would appreciate, yet Walsingham, even more than Burghley, felt there could be no security while the Queen of Scots, a Clytemnestra who had killed a husband and committed adultery, still breathed. Talks of any negotiations with her were useless in his view because she could never keep her word and his spies assured him that at the very moment when she was

TOP Robert Dudley,
Earl of Leicester,
Elizabeth's first and
greatest favourite, in a
miniature painted by
Nicholas Hilliard in 1576.
He lost favour temporarily
following his marriage to
Lettice Knollys, but he was
soon able to re-establish
himself at court. In 1587,
Elizabeth appointed him
commander of her army
in the Netherlands, to help
the Dutch against the
Spanish.

BOTTOM Sir Christopher
Hatton, one of Elizabeth's
favourite courtiers. She
nicknamed him her 'Lids'
and in 1587 she made him
her Lord Chancellor. In
the miniature, his robes
and symbols of office
are shown.

solemnly declaring that she would prefer to die a prisoner than run away with shame, she was up to her eyes in intrigues.

Walter Raleigh, the West Countryman, owed his début at court in the winter of 1581 to three very different factors: his mother was a Champernowne, so that Kate Ashley of fond memory was his great aunt; the Queen, nineteen years his senior, appreciated his intellect no less than his appearance and manner; while service in Ireland had made him something of an expert on the difficult situation there. If the last was the immediate cause of his coming to court, the other two factors weighed most with Elizabeth, who excused him his return to his regiment on the grounds that she needed him at court. By now Leicester had remarried, Alençon was departing for Flanders and Essex was but a boy of fifteen. Raleigh was an unconventional adventurer who had been a soldier of fortune in France before he seized the opportunity of service in Ireland, and now England lay almost at his feet. His head was full of ambitious schemes for founding colonies, of strange ideas about the deity, and of stanzas of pure poetic vision. It was the manysidedness of the man that appealed to Elizabeth; here was a courtier close to the specification of Castiglione. He had 'wit' in the full Elizabethan sense of the term, and it was his greatest asset. She called him 'Warter', mocking his Devonian dialect, and then described him as 'the Shepherd of the Ocean', which provoked his apt response that oceans were always ruled by the moon, so she became his 'Cynthia', the cold, chaste moon of the poet's imagination.

> My thoughts are winged with hopes, my lips with love,
> Mount love, unto the Moon's clearest night,
> And say, as she doth in the heaven's move,
> On earth so wanes and waxeth my delight,
> And whisper this but softly in her ears
> Hope oft doth hang the head and trust shed tears.

Compared with Christopher Hatton, Raleigh's rise was meteoric. Soon this rank outsider, with no hint of noble birth, was being regarded by the Queen as 'a kind of oracle, which nettled them all'. She leased him her residence in the Strand, Durham House, on most favourable terms and granted him the valuable monopoly of retailing sweet wines in taverns through-

L*

out the country, though it was not until 1587, when Hatton achieved the Woolsack, that she appointed him to a court office, and Raleigh became Sir Christopher's successor as Captain of the Bodyguard. 'When will you cease to be a beggar?' Elizabeth once asked him, and the reply came pat, 'when you cease to be a benefactress'. Later ages, unable to appreciate the dramatic force of Raleigh's personality, invented incidents to explain his instant favour. There was the reputed affair of his throwing his cloak in the mud for Elizabeth to walk upon, and there was the opportunist's line, scratched, it was said, on a window-pane with the diamond from his ring – 'Fain would I climb, yet fear to fall', which the Queen noted and capped, with the further line, 'If thy heart fail thee, climb not at all.' Raleigh's heart at this stage never failed him. To fill the part destiny had cast for him this 'darling of the English Cleopatra' (as a Jesuit priest termed him) dressed in the most resplendent raiment; the pearls in his shoes alone were worth perhaps £6,000. Tarleton, the court comedian, dared allege, 'The Knave commands the Queen', and everyone knew whom he meant, for after Raleigh was knighted on Twelfth Night 1585 he was reckoned 'the best hated man of the world'. Hatton, abject that a younger rival should overtake him, sent Elizabeth fresh tokens of devotion – a tiny gold bucket and a jewelled 'fish prison', both alluding to her new-found 'Water' – and she hastened to write back that the 'Water' could not content her nearly so well as her 'Sheep'.

For ten years Raleigh was prime favourite and the Queen was said 'to love this gentleman now beyond all others', yet it was no more than fascination that he aroused. Elizabeth needed his adoration, needed to be reminded of his unswerving devotion to her, as a defence against time and loneliness, but she could not repay him in the coin he wanted. Her eyes, he wrote, had set his fancy on fire, her dainty hands had conquered his desire.

> O eyes that pierce our hearts without remorse,
> O hairs of right that wear a royal crown,
> O hands that conquer more than Caesar's force
> O wit that turns huge kingdoms upside down!
> Then Love, be judge, what heart may thee withstand!
> Such eyes, such hair, such wit, and such a hand!

Sir Walter Raleigh, who
first appeared at court in
1581. His wit and
adventurous spirit
attracted the Queen, and
he quickly established
himself as a favourite. In
this portrait he is shown
with his son, also
called Walter.

Elizabeth's eyes still pierced imperiously and her lovely hands made every gesture significant, but at fifty her hair, faded and already thinning, was discreetly covered by an auburn wig. Certainly, it was the crown that she wore that Raleigh's imagination fed upon, but he could not in all honesty remain in love with its wearer regardless of her age and appearance. The quality he really appreciated was her wit, for he found her a companionable spirit – a woman of intellect who was more than a blue-stocking – fully able to appreciate his own intellectual qualities. She had refused to let him venture to the New World to found an English settlement, but gave her patronage to his Roanoke expedition by accepting his suggestion that the colony should be named 'Virginia' after her. She lent her name to a courtier's dreams, but refused to let him turn them into reality.

In the end Raleigh, no more than Leicester, could remain a passive worshipper of his moon goddess. Then came disillusion. As soon as he found real happiness in a woman able to reciprocate his love – Bess Throckmorton – then they were both banished from court. The bitterness flavours all his later poems, for he had pierced the tinsel (as Essex was to) and seen the old maid on the throne with an auburn wig and a wrinkled face. His marriage with Bess Throckmorton of the Queen's Chamber in 1592, when she was five months with child, snuffed out his career at court like one of his own tobacco pipes. He wrote to Robert Cecil in high strain from the Tower, bemoaning his fate: 'My heart was never broken till this day, that I hear the Queen goes away so far off, whom I have followed so many years with so great love and desire, in so many journeys, and am now left behind her, in a dark prison all alone ...' It was written for the Queen's eye, and if she were shown the letter it made not the slightest difference to Raleigh's case. At that moment he was writing for himself alone his harsh poem *The Lie*:

> Say to the Court it glows,
> And shines like rotten wood.
> Say to the Church it shows
> What's good and doth no good.
> If Church and Court reply,
> Then give them both the lie.

'*My heart was never broken till this day*'

Tell potentates they live
Acting by others' action,
Not loved unless they give,
Not strong but by affection,
If potentates reply,
Give potentates the lie.

On Raleigh's estimation, Elizabeth had failed him; on her's his behaviour was beyond forgiveness.

The assassination of William the Silent by a Catholic fanatic, who imagined that the death of the Dutch leader would provoke the collapse of the revolt, led Walsingham to devise a novel pledge of allegiance, the Bond of Association, in which all Elizabeth's subjects might join in a solemn undertaking to defend her person, and if this failed, to avenge her death. To make doubly sure the revised version included an undertaking that the signatories would never accept as sovereign 'any such pretended successor by whom, or for whom, any such detestable act shall be attempted'; such a claimant would automatically be put to death. Thousands of signatures were soon collected. When Parliament made the Association statutory the Queen objected to what she regarded as tyrannicide with a vengeance, for she refused to countenance a situation in which Mary was to be *automatically* guilty of any plot against her and she told the fanatically loyal Commons, out for Mary's blood, that their concern for her own safety was more than she deserved. She did not want any claimant to the succession to be punished without a trial before commissioners appointed by her and was firm that the penalties should not extend, in Mary's case, to her son James VI unless, of course, he were personally implicated in the conspiracy. After much argument her wishes were met.

Mary, the focus of discontent, was moved from Sheffield Castle to Wingfield in Derbyshire, and at the beginning of 1585 was sent even further south to Tutbury in Staffordshire, where much stricter precautions were taken. Instead of the easy-going Earl of Shrewsbury she had to endure the guardianship first of the precise Sir Ralph Sadler and then of the straight-laced Puritan Sir Amyas Paulet. She had been forbidden to send or receive letters since the discovery of the Throckmorton plot, yet new conspiracies were afoot and Walsingham kept up his ceaseless vigilance. A Catholic exile named Robert Gifford, who had landed in Sussex, was found to be carrying a letter of introduction to Mary and since the man's parents lived near Tutbury he would have been ideally placed for communicating with the royal prisoner. Walsingham won him over to assist in betraying Mary and he was told to inform the French embassy that he had devised a foolproof scheme for passing letters to her. A brewer from Burton-on-Trent, who made regular deliveries of beer to Tutbury, and then to Chartley, where Mary's household had been temporarily removed, was to use barrels with a water-tight container for conveying letters. Mauvissière, the French ambassador, sent a trial letter by this means and duly received Mary's reply. Nearby Walsingham installed his cipher expert, Phelippes, who was soon reading all the correspondence for Mary that had been piling up in the French embassy, but there was nothing really incriminating. After seven months came a letter from the Catholic Anthony Babington, once a page in Shrewsbury's household, who had been persuaded to take part in a further plot and he now proudly revealed the details to Mary, and asked for her approval to the sequence of operations. Overjoyed to learn of fresh efforts for her release Mary replied; she would prefer Elizabeth's assassination to precede her own rescue and in saying as much unequivocally endorsed the scheme, placing herself under the terms of the 1585 Act for the Queen's safety. Thirty years earlier, when messages from Wyatt reached her, the young Elizabeth at Hatfield had committed nothing to paper, but Mary had now signed away her life. Soon Phelippes was deciphering letters from Spain showing that Philip was preparing a great armada to play its part in 'the setting of Your Majesty at liberty'.

Secretary Walsingham kept the cards close to his chest and indeed Elizabeth had only indirectly come to hear of the affair. Babington had recorded the names of his companions in crime, who included the son of the Queen's under-treasurer and a servant of Hatton's. All were eventually caught, yet Elizabeth ordered Burghley to see that at their treason trial nothing should come out which would incriminate Mary. She could not, however, escape from her duties under the Act requiring her to appoint commissioners to investigate Mary's part in the conspiracy and pronounce sentence. For eighteen years she had procrastinated over Mary's fate, and she would try to shirk the issue even now – not because she doubted her guilt in Darnley's murder or the authenticity of the Casket Letters any more than her complicity in Babington's plot, but because Mary was like herself an anointed Queen, her own kinswoman and nearest heir to her throne.

During this crisis Elizabeth remained emotionally disturbed and she missed Leicester, who was commanding her army in the Netherlands. She refused to send Mary to the Tower like a common traitor but at last agreed to move her from Chartley to Fotheringhay in Northamptonshire. Burghley persuaded her that if she summoned Parliament she could share the burden of responsibility. She agreed to this and said she would open the sessions in person, though when the time came she absented herself, as she did not want to appear, she said, as presiding judge over the proceedings against her cousin. She wrote now to the

The trial of Mary Queen of Scots from a contemporary drawing. The trial took place in the hall at Fotheringhay Castle in October 1586. The commission of twenty-four peers and Privy Councillors appointed to investigate Mary's guilt included her jailor, Shrewsbury.

Scottish Queen, aware she was 'void of all remorse or conscience', warning her of the coming trial according to the law of the land in which she had lived 'under our protection'. Mary at first refused to plead before the commissioners at Fotheringhay, so they wrote for guidance and Elizabeth told them they must indeed proceed with the trial, but were not to pronounce sentence without reference to her. After the usual rehearsal of the evidence, which dominated state trials, the judges reassembled in the Star Chamber to review the case and pronounce Mary 'an imaginer and compasser of Her Majesty's destruction'. Lords and Commons held their own review of the affair showing Mary to be the mainspring of every conspiracy against Protestant England because she was by nationality a Scot, by upbringing French and in practice Spanish. A Parliamentary deputation waited on Elizabeth at Richmond, petitioning that Mary should pay the extreme penalty, but she reminded them that the Act of 1585 for her safety was grounded in her people's spontaneous Bond of Association. Was there no other way than execution? A second deputation listened to a characteristic speech. 'I was not simply trained up, nor in my youth spent my time altogether idly; and yet when I came to the throne, then I entered first into the school of experience.' She talked of her justice and how in her time she had pardoned rebels; and yet, as her Councillors feared, she ended on a terrifying note of indecision: 'Pray you to accept my thankfulness, excuse my doubtfulness and take in good part my answer answerless ...' Council and Parliament pressed her further in the following weeks to sign the death warrant that had been prepared.

Without warning on 1 February 1587 she ordered Secretary Davison to bring her the warrant and, after reading it through, signed it, telling him to take it to the Lord Chancellor and also to tell Walsingham, who was ill, for the news would put him on his feet again. The world would see, she said, there had been nothing hasty about Mary's death, yet she had hoped better things of Paulet, Mary's guardian, who could so readily still ease her of her public burden. Both Leicester and Archbishop Whitgift had suggested Mary might be poisoned or suffocated during her sleep and now Elizabeth called for the men at Fotheringhay to do no more than they had volunteered under the Bond of Association. It was pitiful that Elizabeth should be

'Take in good part my answer answerless'

so overwrought as to ask Paulet to commit judicial murder, for there was justification enough in publicly executing Mary for undoubted crimes under the laws of England. When Paulet stoutly refused to act in a secret way she chided him for his 'daintiness'. Burghley and others predicted the Queen would try to retract, so they acted the moment the warrant had been signed. At a hastily called meeting her Councillors shared the responsibility for sending the warrant to Fotheringhay without further reference to the Queen, and as a result Mary was executed on 8 February. She had spent the last evening busy at her correspondence, and at 6 a.m. rose to hand over her will, distribute purses to her servants and take her leave of them

A contemporary painting of dancing at court, traditionally said to represent Elizabeth dancing with Robert Dudley.

173

before going into her little oratory to pray before the crucifix. A wooden stage had been erected in the centre of the great hall in Fotheringhay where three hundred spectators had gathered, with the Earls of Shewsbury and Kent. At about 9.30 a.m. they saw the entry of the tall regal figure, utterly composed, walking to her death at the age of forty-four; Mary was dressed in black except for her veil and peaked head-dress. Led to the stage she listened to the reading of the royal commission for the execution, but dispensed with the administrations of the Dean of Peterborough: 'Mr Dean, I am settled in the ancient Catholic Roman religion', she reminded him, 'and mind to spend my blood in defence of it.' After prayers, she forgave her executioner as of custom and was helped to undress down to her dark red petticoat and a satin bodice with a neckline cut down low at the back, and put on a pair of red sleeves, so that she appeared in the colour of martyrdom in the liturgy of the Catholic Church. Fearlessly, she laid her head on the block, praying constantly. The first blow of the axe missed her neck, but the second severed it, and at once the executioner held on high the dead Queen's head, shouting out the traditional 'God save the Queen'. However, the head fell from his hand, leaving him holding an auburn wig, while Mary's own hair was found to everybody's astonishment to be quite grey and cut short. No less poignant was the emergence from the long petticoat of a pet Skye terrier that had stayed by his mistress until the end. 'So perish all the Queen's enemies' commented the Dean to the crowd, to which Kent added 'Amen', but Shrewsbury was too moved to speak. Shrewsbury's son rode at once to court to report the execution of the warrant. As soon as he did this, the ports were closed to delay the news of Mary's death reaching Europe.

Elizabeth can hardly have expected her Councillors to have acted otherwise. For weeks they had been demanding the execution of the law and now the warrant bore her signature they would not dawdle. But when she heard of Mary's execution she was more angry than at any time in her life; part was genuine anger – that the ten Councillors had been bold enough to take the decision that she had shrunk from – part was feigned, as a defence against foreign protests. Hatton was in bad odour, Davison was put in the Tower and Burghley banned from court, while the Lord Chancellor, Whitgift and the Chief

Justice were to investigate the action of the Council, though in fact none of the ten Councillors concerned revealed their secret oaths to keep Elizabeth ignorant of what was happening until after Mary's death. Davison was to become the chief scapegoat for the Queen's conscience, enduring prison and an exceptionally heavy fine – his career was in shreds. In the end the safety of the state came first and, however secure Mary's prison, the plots against Elizabeth would continue as long as she breathed. Mary's death marked the final failure of the Catholic revival, for it declared unmistakably that England was a Protestant realm. The popularity of the execution enhanced her reputation and, against her will, Elizabeth became the hope of the Protestant world. In Rome Pope Sixtus V, ignorant of her doubts, had no illusions about the significance of the dignified scene at Fotheringhay and he could not but admire Elizabeth, as Don John of Austria had done: 'What a valiant woman. She braves the two greatest Kings [France and Spain] by land and sea .... It is a pity that Elizabeth and I cannot marry; our children would have ruled the whole world.' As a final dynastic gesture Mary had written to Spain assigning to Philip II her presumptive right to the English throne and Philip, painfully aware that Spain was already fighting England in the Netherlands and on the high seas, pledged himself to undertake a holy crusade against the heretical Queen.

Elizabeth abhorred war for its inhumanity and waste, yet even before Fotheringhay she had seen that an open war with Spain was inevitable. After William the Silent's assassination the Dutch cause seemed lost; Brussels and Antwerp fell and the Duke of Parma looked invincible. Then, casting an even darker shadow over Europe, Henry Duke of Guise signed a treaty in January 1585 with Spain for a Holy League to exclude the rightful heir, the Huguenot Henry of Navarre, from the French succession. Thus England's Treaty of Blois with France was overturned. In desperation the Dutch turned to Elizabeth offering her the sovereignty of their provinces if she would supply soldiers and money to halt Parma's advance. She rejected such terms for, as a Queen, she knew she could not affront Philip II by accepting the allegiance of his rebel subjects and she feared involving England in a long, costly war. Instead of

'Our children would have ruled the whole world.'

Den VIII february werde onthalsi Maria
Stuart Schots Coninginne s texxende gconis Catho-
lyck hebbende gesocht veel onxusten aen te xichten haex schoy
mee ter te maecken van Engelant dxoelck haex vanden Raet
ofte parlement volcomelyck swexde vextoont, Anno.1587.
Metren XIII fol. XIII. en XIIII. b.

A coloured drawing of the execution of Mary Queen of Scots, which took place at Fotheringhay on 8 February 1587. A wooden stage was erected in the great hall, and the Earls of Shrewsbury and Kent are shown presiding over the ceremony.

sovereignty she hit on the apt formula of taking the Dutch people under her protection and promised to send an army at her own cost under a high-ranking commander, while the Estates were to allow English occupation of two 'cautionary' towns, Flushing and Brill. What 'protection' meant was spelt out in her Declaration issued to the courts of Europe in the middle of August 1585. She made quite plain that she had not intervened for territorial gain, but to ensure the stability of Europe and the security of England, and as protector she would see that the Dutch recovered their traditional freedom that had been lost under Spanish tyranny. This document was a challenge to Philip II – unlike the activities of the marauders in the New World – which he could not ignore. Not so long before,

176

she had told the Spanish ambassador: 'I am more afraid of making a fault in my Latin than of the Kings of Spain, France, Scotland, or the whole house of Guise and all their confederates. I have the heart of a man, not a woman, and I am not afraid of anything.' England was to remain at war for the rest of her reign and during those seventeen years achieved an internal unity and national consciousness which enhanced Elizabeth's reputation on all sides. Certainly, in the first years, the war was popular with her subjects. The cream of the nation's manhood, who had been fighting for the Dutch cause as volunteers since 1569, were delighted at the Queen's decision and seamen dreamt of rich prizes.

As always, when there was some special responsibility to be borne, she thought of Leicester. He was appointed commander of the army to be sent to the Netherlands, though she was most reluctant to let him go and he no less reluctant to take up a post where his authority would be limited by the Dutch Council as well as by instructions from Whitehall. He hoped Elizabeth would never again put a man in his difficult position, 'yet I will do what I can for her and her country'. When a delegation came to offer him the absolute government of Holland, Zeeland and two other provinces he foolishly accepted, hoping this would ease his problems. Elizabeth was furious, as he should have predicted, shouting that the hand which had raised up Robert Dudley could beat him to dust and she required him immediately to renounce the high-flown title of 'His Excellency the Captain General', obeying the instructions Heneage brought over 'at his uttermost peril'. The campaign proper was not going well; Parma, Philip's general, was the finest soldier in Europe, leading a seasoned, professional army, while the English troops were essentially amateurs, inexperienced in the difficulties of a land campaign on the Continent, and distrustful of their Dutch comrades-in-arms. At best the war would end in stalemate and the morale of England was saved only by Sir Philip Sydney's wound at Zutphen. Overnight this chivalrous man became a national hero and was given a state funeral in St Paul's, an honour not again accorded to an Englishman until Nelson. Leicester, who quarrelled badly with Prince Maurice of Nassau, the ablest Dutch soldier, was in poor health and eager to be home. He was relieved that by June Elizabeth's temper had

LEFT Sir Philip Sydney, the epitome of chivalry at the Elizabethan court. He went to the Nether-lands with Leicester to aid the Dutch against the Duke of Parma. He was mortally wounded at the battle of Zutphen, where his fame became legendary by his giving the water intended for him to a dying soldier.

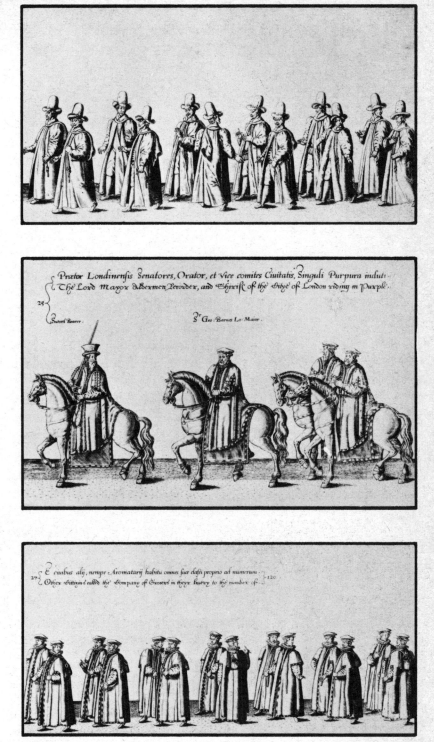

RIGHT Sydney became a national hero, and was given a state funeral in St Paul's Cathedral – an un-precedented honour. These engravings show the citizens of London taking part in the funeral procession.

abated: 'Rob', she wrote, 'I am afraid you will suppose by my wandering writings that a midsummer moon hath taken large possession of my brains this month ...' By November he was allowed home to take the waters at Bath, then he had to return to his command in 1587 with instructions to persuade the Dutch to join in making fresh peace overtures. Leicester's heart was no more in negotiating with Parma than in conducting a land campaign, and by Christmas Lord Willoughby succeeded him and he could return to court for good.

If England's military machine creaked, the navy was in superb shape, thanks largely to Sir John Hawkins who, with an imaginative construction programme, had made the fleet a fine instrument of war and, by his reform of the dockyards, had saved the Queen money at the same time. Though the main fleet consisted of only twenty-five vessels of the first class, all were in splendid trim, with their long-range guns, and the smaller galleons Hawkins had devised were easy to handle and could stay at sea for long periods. Behind the men-of-war lay a very considerable reserve of merchantmen, whose owners could be relied upon to defend the coasts in a crisis, just as some of them had eagerly joined the expeditions for plundering Spanish ships and settlements west of 'the Line'. During the breathing-space that Elizabeth's diplomacy had won there had been intense activity on many fronts that amounted to 'war production'. National resources were being exploited, inventiveness was being rewarded. German engineers were prospecting for metals, Huguenots from Brittany were spreading knowledge of their craft of sailmaking, and of a truth a remarkable industrial revolution was in train; the enthusiasm for making the realm self-sufficient came from above, but Elizabeth's subjects responded to her challenge. For a decade English merchants had been enjoying great prosperity, taking advantage of the difficulties of rival trading nations, freeing themselves from the old dependence on Antwerp by forging new, direct links with markets from the Baltic to the Levant, so that by the time Antwerp had fallen to Parma, London was already an international port. The last of the great series of corporate trading companies was the East India Company, chartered by the Queen on the last day of the century and destined to found an empire in India. While Philip II had relied

'I am more afraid of making a fault in my Latin than of the Kings of Spain, France, Scotland'

for his wealth on the gold and silver from his American conquests, with disastrous results, Elizabeth's subjects largely earned their foreign currency by exporting cloth to all European countries, not only the traditional broadcloths and worsteds but the 'new draperies' that Dutch and Walloon refugees had brought to East Anglia.

The Queen shared hardly at all in this new prosperity from foreign trade, for taxation remained light, but ever since 1566 she had invested in the buccaneering expeditions of bolder spirits in American waters. Drake returned from his raid on Nombre de Dios in 1572 with a fortune, and encouraged Elizabeth to take more shares than she could afford in his voyage round the world that produced an even more handsome dividend. In 1585, with the breach with Spain, she lent Drake £10,000 and two men-of-war for his attack on Santo Diego and Cartagena. Englishmen had refused to accept the papal ruling that reserved to Spain all lands west of the Azores and north of the Tropic of Capricorn ('the Line'), so depredations such as Drake's were justified on grounds of religious fervour and patriotic zeal no less than on those of commercial prudence. Hakluyt's *Principal Navigations*, telling the story of these remarkable voyages, became as much a best-seller with later Elizabethans as Foxe's *Book of Martyrs* had been with their fathers.

With Elizabeth's open intervention in the Netherlands and her execution of Mary Queen of Scots, Philip ii in 1587 decided he could not wait until the Dutch provinces had been reconquered before attacking England. He had never forgotten or forgiven her refusal to marry him, the obvious husband, and each succeeding year there had been fresh slights – treating his ambassadors with utter rudeness, encouraging attacks on Spanish shipping, aiding the Dutch rebels with loans and transferring England's traditional allegiance from the Habsburgs to the rival House of Valois. This heretic of a sister-in-law, by daring to defy the Pope, had placed herself beyond the pale, and as Philip scrutinised the reports reaching the Escorial he decided to undertake a holy enterprise to carry out the papal deposition of 1570 and, as Mary's 'heir', he would ascend the English throne himself. He was sure 25,000 English Catholics would rise to welcome Parma's army of liberation which would cross from Flanders, while a great armada held the narrow seas.

A map of 1588, showing
the preparations made on
the Thames against a
projected Spanish invasion.
Philip II planned that
Parma, in Flanders, should
send over the army of
invasion and thus the
south-east part of England
was in an extremely
vulnerable position.

England prepared for invasion by training the militia in the
counties and establishing a system of beacons along the head-
lands to give warning of the enemy's approach. To launch an
attack on the galleons assembled in Spanish harbours seemed the
best method of defence and so, in the spring of 1587, Drake led
a devastating raid on Cadiz, at the end of which he took and
burned great quantities of empty barrels, that were to be used
for victualling the fleet, and captured a great Portuguese vessel
with £140,000 of treasure. The 'singeing of the King of Spain's
beard' meant that the sailing of the Armada was postponed.
Elizabeth required her wealthier subjects to contribute to a
forced loan and ordered the coastal towns to fit out ships for
defence since her revenue of 'chested treasure' was running out
and there was not the time to summon a Parliament to vote
supplies to be assessed and collected in the usual cumbersome
way.

Philip II in the Escorial, usually so reluctant to make decisions,
pushed ahead against professional advice; in the end the victualling arrangements had to be skimped and the number of soldiers
to be transported in the fleet was heavily reduced so that Parma
in Flanders would have to furnish the entire invading army.
The Marquis of Santa Cruz, who had drawn up the original
plans, had died and now the Duke of Medina Sidonia, a grandee
without experience afloat, found to his dismay that he was to be
Philip's admiral; he proved himself brave and level-headed, even
in the face of persistent sea sickness. Pope Sixtus V, though he
withheld financial support, gave his blessing to the 'Enterprise
of England' and every man in the fleet took the sacrament before
sailing. A storm had played havoc with many vessels as they
moved on from Lisbon to Corunna, but Philip insisted there
could be no further delays while shipwrights thoroughly
repaired the damage. The Armada left Corunna on 12 July
1588 and a week later sighted the Lizard.

Charles Howard of
Effingham, later 1st Earl of
Nottingham, the Queen's
cousin. She appointed
Howard to command her
fleet against the Spanish
Armada.

The Queen appointed Lord Howard of Effingham to command her fleet and as a man of strong personality he could keep the unruly seadogs, Drake, Hawkins and Frobisher, in their places. Howard's main fleet was based at Queenborough to defend the Thames approaches; from Dover, Lord Henry Seymour patrolled the Straits, while Drake was stationed at Plymouth eager for action. In May Howard moved his ships to join Drake's in Plymouth Sound, yet for some weeks Elizabeth would not allow them to go in search of the enemy because she was afraid the Armada might elude them and England would be defenceless. Then she grudgingly allowed them to take on victuals for an expedition and soon ninety ships were hastening towards the Bay of Biscay, though they were forced to return to base when the wind shifted to the south, on the very day that Medina Sidonia had left Corunna. On 19 July came news that the Armada had been seen off the Scillies so the English fleet left Plymouth Sound on the evening tide to anchor in deep water and prepare to take up position to the south of the enemy. The Spanish admiral had formed his fleet into a great crescent, with the strongest galleons at the points and flanks so that they seemed to Howard an impregnable formation 'with lofty towers, castlelike, in front like a crescent moon'. For five days the two fleets moved in stately fashion up the English Channel, but it was stalemate; neither side could get to grips with its opponent and they were both running short of ammunition.

On 27 July Medina Sidonia safely brought his fleet to anchor off Calais, yet Parma had no flat-bottomed craft available to transport his army, camped on the dunes, to the anchorage. Howard, unable to bring his ships within firing range of the enemy, called a council of war at which the suggestion was made to send in fire ships. Once Drake had volunteered to use his own vessel other offers quickly came. These fire ships were loaded with tar and anything that would burn and were double-shotted so that they would explode from the great heat. Soon after midnight they drifted, lashed together, across to the anchorage and in great confusion the Spanish vessels cut their cables and sailed out to sea. At dawn Howard divided his ships to give chase; and in the close fighting off Gravelines the English showed their superiority in handling their craft. Squalls and blinding rain saved the Armada from certain defeat and when

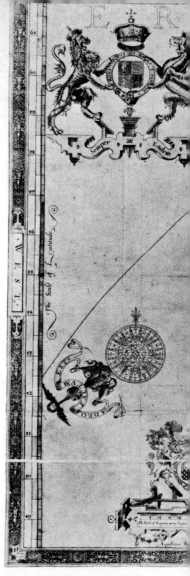

A map of the British Isles in 1588, showing the course of the Spanish fleet. In the bottom right-hand corner the English and Spanish fleets are depicted off Calais, where Drake's fire-ships created havoc. Further up, Howard is shown pursuing the Spanish fleet off the coast of Holland. Medina Sidonia, the Spanish commander, decided to

make for the deep water of the North Sea, and to sail westward around the British Isles back to Spain. North of Berwick, Howard ceased to pursue and the Spanish fleet can be traced around the Orkneys and Shetlands and the west of Ireland. Storms, disease and hunger depleted the fleet, so that only sixty-seven ships reached Spain.

the visibility improved Howard pursued the enemy along the Netherlands coast. Early on 30 July, when it seemed likely that they would be driven on the lee shore of the Zeeland sands, the wind backed to west-south-west, to enable Medina Sidonia to make for the deep water of the North Sea. He decided in the light of his casualties, that if the wind held he would have to sail westward around the British Isles to make for home, but if the wind should change he could attempt to force his way through the Straits of Dover to take an English port. The wind held, so the Armada began its long homeward voyage, sailing up the east coast of England and Scotland, around the Orkneys and Shetlands and the west of Ireland, with insufficient food and water. Howard pursued them to the north of Berwick and then let them go. Seventeen of the galleons broke away from the fleet to attempt to make Irish ports in search of food, but most foundered. The remaining sixty-seven limped home, and when Medina Sidonia reached Santander on 13 September he was delirious with dysentery and many of his men had died from typhus or scurvy.

In London in early August there was confusion about the course of the battle. Leicester, the Lieutenant General for the defence of the realm, had assembled his army at Tilbury. Elizabeth was dismayed at being shut in by guards at St James's (where her sister had taken refuge as Wyatt marched on London) for she wanted to be in the midst of things. Leicester thought it too dangerous for her to visit the coast but agreed to let her come to Tilbury camp, where she rode through the ranks wearing steel armour 'like some Amazonian empress'. Next day she returned to Tilbury and, with rumours that Parma was embarking his army, she decided to give her troops a rousing speech:

> Let tyrants fear. I have always so behaved myself that, under God, I have placed my chiefest strength and goodwill in the loyal hearts and goodwill of my subjects; and therefore I am come amongst you, as you see, at this time, not for my recreation and disport, but being resolved in the midst and heat of the battle to live or die amongst you all; to lay down for God, my kingdom and for my people, my honour and my blood, even in the dust. I know I have but the body of a weak and feeble woman: but I have the heart and stomach of a king – and a king of England too – and think it foul scorn that Parma or Spain or any Prince of Europe should dare to invade the borders of my realm ...

Then she praised Leicester's qualities of leadership and convinced her hearers they would soon have 'a famous victory'. There were incredible expressions of loyalty to her. The Earl thought her heroic speech would stiffen the weakest man in his army to match the proudest Spaniard.

Ignorant of the fact that Parma's chances had evaporated once the fire ships had scattered the Armada, Elizabeth stayed near the camp for a week, feeling that honour demanded that she should be with her men, but once the danger had passed she returned to London to celebrate. She toyed with the idea of making Leicester her viceroy, though Burghley and Hatton thought ill

'I have the heart and stomach of a king—and a king of England too'

A playing card of the early seventeenth century, showing Leicester as Lieutenant General for the defence of the realm, in August 1588. He assembled his army at Tilbury ready to encounter Parma, should he disembark from the Low Countries.

of this. Soon the fleet was laid up and the army disbanded to save the wages' bill, and seamen dying from typhus were cheated of their pay. There was a great review in the tiltyard at Whitehall, organised by Leicester's stepson, Essex, and soon there were thanksgiving services, medals and paintings all enthroning the 'Protestant Wind'. Throughout Europe, indeed, the English victory was ascribed to divine intervention. The defeat of the Armada was a decisive event in that it checked the colossus of Spain, which had grown enormous from Lepanto, the conquest of Portugal and the successes of Parma in the Netherlands, and accordingly the Protestant cause found a new heart; the world had not ended after all, with the Massacre of St Bartholomew or the murder of William of Orange.

Leicester had shared in the immediate triumphs at court, though he felt ill and soon left to take the waters at Buxton. On the way he stayed at Rycote, in the room Lady Norris usually kept for the Queen's visits, and from there he wrote to her, to ask after her health, 'being the chiefest thing in the world I do pray for', and to tell her that the medicine she gave him was doing him good. 'I humbly kiss your foot, from your old lodging at Rycote, this Thursday morning, by Your Majesty's most faithful and obedient servant, R. Leycester.' Yet within the week he had died and Elizabeth became so overwhelmed with grief that she locked herself in her room, refusing to see anyone until, it is said, some of her Councillors risked ordering the door to be broken in. 'Sweet Robin', the man she had been emotionally bound to for thirty years was no more and his death soured the fruits of victory. The intensity of her feelings for Dudley came out after she, too, had died, when among her most treasured keepsakes locked in a casket by her bed was his final letter from Rycote with her own note in a shaking hand 'His last letter'.

Living into old age brought cruel losses – a woman's looks as well as the death of her oldest friends. The grandeur of the series of Armada portraits and the painting of Elizabeth standing on the map of England, her feet on Oxfordshire (1592) largely conceal the ravages that time had made upon her face and physique. Gloriana, superb in her ruff, farthingale and jewels, was nearing sixty; an auburn wig hid her thinning hair, white powder and paint masked her wrinkles. Of all her features her

The Thankfull
Remembrance of 1588.
RIGHT The fire ships of
the English fleet wreak
havoc amongst the
Spanish galleons. On land,
the Queen and her soldiers
watch, while behind stand
the lighted beacons which
warned the country of the
threat of the Spaniards.
BELOW The thanksgiving
service at St Paul's
following the destruction
of the Spanish fleet. The
Earl of Essex organised a
great review in the tiltyard
at Whitehall to give thanks
for the 'Protestant' Wind'.

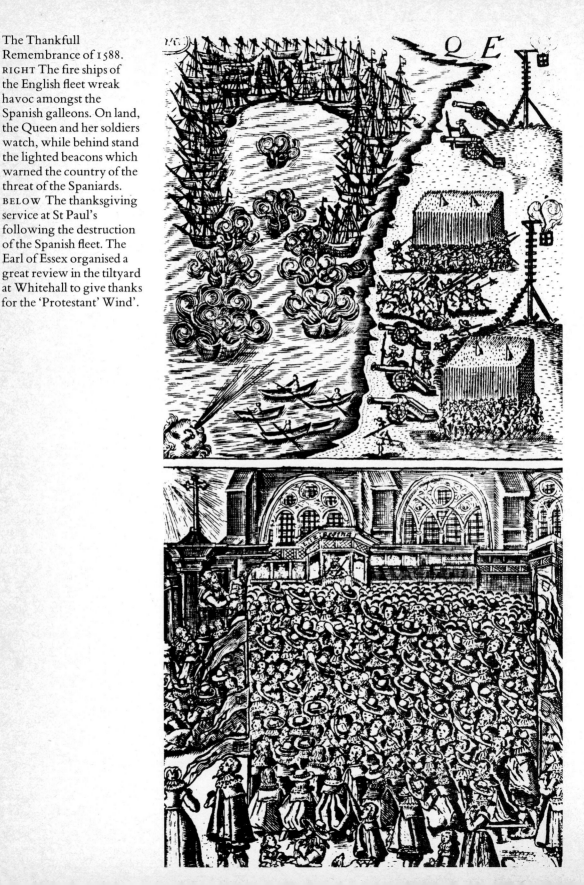

Robert Dudley did not
long survive the triumph
over the Spanish Armada.
On his way to Buxton, he
stayed at Rycote with Lady
Norris and wrote his last
letter to the Queen, signed
'by your Majesty's most
faithful and obedient
servant. R. Leycester.'
A week later he was dead
and Elizabeth had lost her
closest friend.

hands remained beautiful, and she knew how to use them to best advantage. She was conscious of being over-weight, suffered torments from toothache, and tired more easily than she admitted. But artificial aids could not make good the losses from within her family circle at court. In 1591 Hatton was mortally ill at Ely Place by Hatton Garden, and she visited him bringing 'cordial broths' for him to sip and tried to take his mind off death and the thought of the money he owed her. As he put it, she had fished for men's souls with so sweet a bait that 'no one could escape her network'; she had caught many poor fish – even himself – 'who little knew what snare was laid for them'. Christopher Hatton alone among her favourites had stayed single for her sake and now as Lord Chancellor of England he took leave of his great fisherman. For Elizabeth the unease of old age, as she approached the grand climacteric, was made tolerable by the affection of her subjects and by the person of young Essex, in that order.

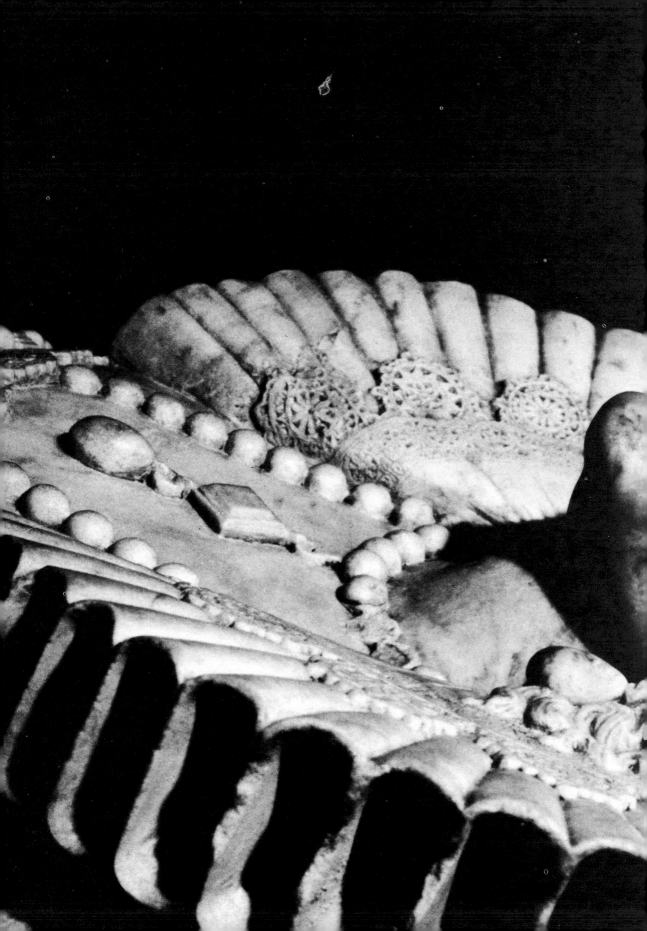

8 Knave, Queen, King
1591-1603

THE RANKS AT COURT were thinning out, and each death of one of the older generation of royal servants snapped another link with the past. Hunsdon, who had routed the rebels under Dacre, Sir Francis Knollys, Treasurer of the household and grandfather of Essex, and the Puritan Huntingdon with Plantagenet blood, all died in a matter of months. The death of Blanche Parry of the Privy Chamber, a close companion of the Queen for more years than she cared to remember, though latterly blind and frail, moved her even more and she ordered her to be buried. with the dignity of a baroness. It was unbelievably tactless of Bishop Rudde of St David's to have preached at such a time on the text 'Lord, teach us to number our days', reminding the Queen that she was sixty-three, which by his strange computation of mystical numbers he pronounced as her 'climacterial year'. Seeing her scowls the Bishop extricated himself as best he could – there was no doubt she would pass this year and many more, he said; but Elizabeth advised him to keep his arithmetic to himself, for 'I see the greatest clerks are not always the wisest men'. By Tudor standards Elizabeth was indeed old, yet her powers were very far from failing her and she retained a remarkable grip on affairs until her last illness, seven years after the Bishop's unfortunate sermon.

As with most ambitious youths, Robert Devereux, Earl of Essex, had come to court in 1585 to seek his fortune, for his father, more of a soldier than a courtier, had passed on heavy debts and, left to himself by his mother, who speedily married Leicester, he courted the Queen's favour as the surest way of putting his finances in order. But, unlike the others, he had the inestimable advantage of noble birth coupled with wonderful features. With his shock of auburn hair and his striking black eyes, he was as handsome a boy as might have been expected for the son of Lettice Knollys, and the Queen, thirty-four years his senior, warmed to his flattery. As Leicester's stepson, he considered he was being groomed for the succession to principal favourite as of right, and Elizabeth would have been captivated by him quite apart from his connexions with Dudley and the fact that her mother's sister, Mary Boleyn, had been his great-grandmother. At eighteen Essex had won his spurs at Zutphen, where Sir Philip Sydney was mortally wounded, and this gave him a taste for martial glory which he never lost. Just as he could

PREVIOUS PAGES The effigy of Elizabeth from her tomb in Westminster Abbey. The magnificent tomb of white marble which houses both Elizabeth and her half-sister Mary in an uneasy alliance, was made by Maximilian Colt and John de Critz.

192

charm women with wit, flattery and a penetrating glance, so too he had a strange magnetism over men, persuading them he was their natural leader, under whom it would be a privilege to serve, even to death. He was for ever torn between the rival claims of court and military service, balancing his campaign in the Privy Chamber with service in the field or afloat, though once Elizabeth had fallen under his spell she would not easily let him out of her sight. 'At night my lord is at cards, or one game or another with her, that he cometh not to his own lodgings till birds sing in the morning', said Essex's steward while Leicester was still alive. Success came too easily to him and it went to his head so that he remained a spoilt child, utterly self-centred, petulant and unpredictable.

Established favourites felt the tension rise as he entered the room. When Essex boxed Raleigh's ears for being forward, the Queen in turn lost her temper and made snide remarks to the Earl about his mother. 'What comfort can I have to give myself over to the service of a mistress that is in awe of such a man', wrote Essex, still only seventeen. He fled to the coast to find a boat to take him to the Netherlands, where he might find a hero's grave rather than be humiliated by Elizabeth. In desperation she sent a message commanding his return and to appease him made him Master of the Horse. Later, in disobedience to her wishes, he sailed with Drake on the Portugal Expedition in 1589 and her peremptory summons to return could not be served on him for two months. 'Essex, your sudden and undutiful departure from our presence and your place of attendance, you may easily conceive how offensive it is ... Our great favours bestowed on you without deserts hath drawn you thus to neglect and forget your duty.' As he had expected, when he did at last return to court, she readily forgave him, for it was wonderful to have him at her side again. If the Queen smiled on any other man he was quick to take offence. She had rewarded Lord Mountjoy's son, Charles Blount, for an outstanding performance in the tiltyard by sending him a golden queen from her set of chessmen, which he proudly tied to his arm with a ribbon, yet at once Essex laughed at him, saying 'every fool must have a favour'. Blount challenged the Earl to a duel, wounding him in the thigh. Elizabeth hoped this might do him some good – 'By God's death, it was fit that someone or other

OVERLEAF, LEFT Two pen and ink drawings tinted with water colour, showing the campaigns of Hugh Maguire, the Irish chieftain, against the English in the 1590s. The drawings were made by John Thomas, a soldier who took part in the campaigns.
BOTTOM Hugh Maguire was Tyrone's ablest and most courageous lieutenant. He was besieged in Enniskillen Castle in 1592 by Sir Richard Bingham, Elizabeth's Governor of Connaught. Bingham eventually took the castle, but Maguire returned to invest it, and defeated Bingham at the 'Ford of Biscuits' after Bingham lost his food supplies in the river.
TOP Maguire defeated at the battle of Ballishannon in October 1593. The artist has even drawn Maguire's pipers. Maguire was eventually killed in 1600 in an engagement near Cork, while commanding the cavalry in Tyrone's expedition into Munster and Leinster.

OVERLEAF, RIGHT Robert Devereux, 2nd Earl of Essex, a portrait attributed to Marcus Gheeraerts. With his handsome face and fine figure, he dazzled the ageing Queen. Judging from the cut of his beard and his age, the portrait was painted after his return from Cadiz in 1596.

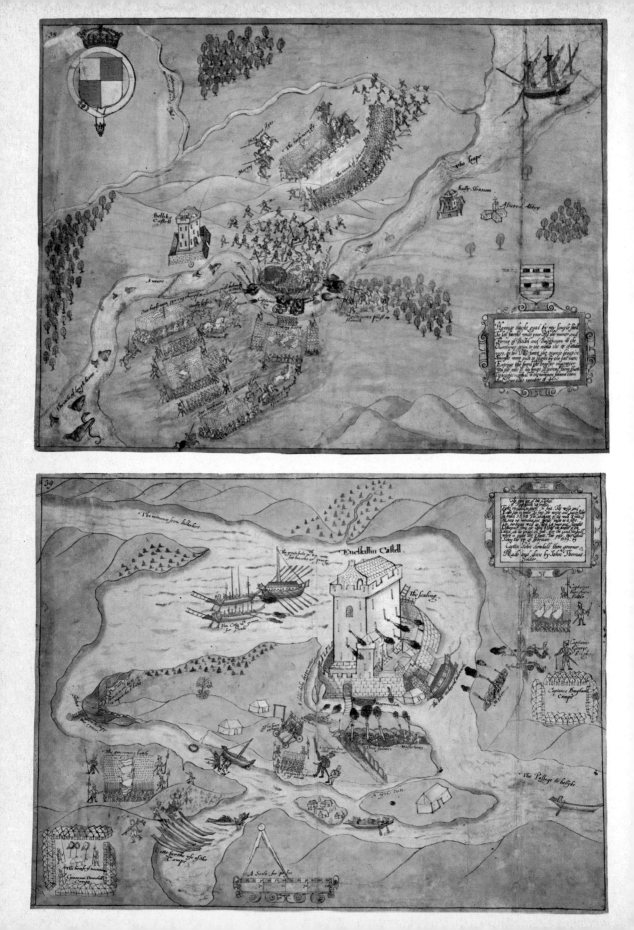

should take him down and teach him better manners, otherwise there would be no rule with him.' She forbade both Essex and Blount to come to court until they had made up their quarrel; and when a few weeks later the Earl issued a challenge to Raleigh, she intervened to prevent a duel. Elizabeth at fifty-six could not hide her pleasure that men should be willing to fight over her, and it was almost like the court of the first year of her reign, when Pickering, Dudley and Arundel had been eager to flash their swords for her.

'*When your Majesty thinks that heaven is too good for me I will not fall like a star*'

But Robert Devereux, the darling of the court, was not going to become emotionally tied to an ageing woman with wrinkles and decayed teeth. Early in 1590 he secretly married Frances, the widow of Philip Sydney, whose father, Walsingham, was in his last days. It could well have been his admiration for his hero's life and death that led him to marry Sydney's widow as the height of chivalrous conduct, for Frances was neither an heiress nor by now a dazzling beauty. By autumn when Frances was great with child, Essex realised he must himself tell the Queen of his marriage, and for once he contrived to handle her with tact. That he had married at all was a personal affront to Elizabeth, yet he had compounded for his fault by choosing a bride far beneath him. By now, however, Elizabeth had become hardened to the behaviour of her favourites whose matrimonial escapades – Hatton apart – had made nonsense of their fervent professions of constancy to their sovereign lady. Essex implored her to let him go to France with an army to help Henry of Navarre in the siege of Rouen, and at his third audience he knelt for two full hours until she gave way. Before long she ordered him home and he protested that she was bent on ruining him. He wanted to achieve some measure of gallant service for her sake, to redeem his honour too, and then 'no cause but a great action of your own may drawn me out of your sight, for the two windows of your Privy Chamber shall be the poles of my sphere ... When Your Majesty thinks that heaven too good for me I will not fall like a star, but be consumed like a vapour by the same Sun that drew me up to such a height'. Elizabeth gave him a reprieve until Christmas when she required his return, and this time he obeyed at once, kissing the hilt of his sword as he stepped aboard the boat to bring him to England. By then Hatton was dead and Raleigh in the Tower for marrying, and perhaps seducing, Bess Throckmorton, Elizabeth's maid-of-honour, and Essex in theory had no rival.

The war against Spain was essentially a naval affair and Essex insisted on having command of various expeditions, especially after the last, fatal voyage of Drake and Hawkins to the Caribbean in 1595–6. Sir John Hawkins on his deathbed had made out a legacy of £2,000 to Elizabeth to recompense her for her losses on the expedition, and Drake went on to make a second attack on Nombre de Dios, but was soon dead from dysentery and so was buried off Porto Bello. Before the Queen heard of the death of her best-loved seamen she was preparing for a combined assault on Cadiz that would make Drake's singeing a minor action in comparison, to make certain that no further Armada could trouble England. Suddenly came news of a crisis much nearer home, for Philip II's new Governor of the Netherlands, the Cardinal Archduke Albert, had launched a surprise attack on Calais; Henry IV of France appealed at once for English aid and Elizabeth could not resist the chance of having an army in Calais again. On Good Friday 1596 she ordered 6,000 men to be ready at Dover in two days to embark under Essex, for she had heard the Cardinal's artillery from Greenwich and realised she must act quickly. Then, as always, she had second thoughts and by the time she agreed to the sailing of the transports, sending Essex a prayer that 'God cover you under His safest wings and let all peril go without your compass', it was too late.

The fact that Calais was now in Spanish hands made her hesitate anew about Cadiz. At one time she cancelled the entire expedition, then she decided to appoint different commanders, but in the end she was wheedled into allowing a fleet of one hundred and twenty sail to leave under Lord Admiral Howard and Essex as joint commanders. She sent the favourite another prayer she had composed that the English victory would be achieved with 'the least loss of English blood' and on 20 June Cadiz was surprised, the galleons destroyed and the city captured. Essex wanted to hold it with a garrison as another Calais, but had been overruled, and when he suggested they wait for the arrival of the plate fleet from America he was again outvoted at a council of war by Howard and Raleigh. Later Elizabeth feared she had been cheated of her share of the rich booty and was to send Sir Anthony Ashley, her financial agent on the voyage, to prison, but her immediate reaction at the victory was spontaneous praise: 'Let the army know I care not so much being Queen as that I am sovereign of such subjects.' Philip II, humiliated by the attack, planned to send the remnant of his fleet against England, but the galleons were scattered in the Bay of Biscay.

Though Raleigh and Essex inevitably quarrelled about who won the laurels of Cadiz, it was that expedition which made the Earl the darling of the adventurers, who had found their feet in warfare and were coming to look on soldiering as a glorious profession, and he headily reciprocated their affection. By now the Queen and numbers of her subjects were tired of the war; not so Essex, who said how much he loved his followers in arms, 'for I find sweetness in their conversation, strong assistance in their employment and happiness in their friendship. I love them for their virtue's sake and for their greatness of mind'. He had become the idol of the people, who drank his health openly, and nodded approvingly when Protestant preachers compared him to Caesar. No other favourite of the Queen's had been popular; Leicester had always been suspect and aloof, Raleigh was mistrusted for being too clever, but Essex courted popularity now and looked to the Queen's patronage to reward his supporters. Francis Bacon, the most intelligent of his following, saw the danger very clearly, comparing the Earl to Icarus who had put on wings made of wax and feathers to fly towards the burning sun with such disastrous consequences. Elizabeth must regard him, said Bacon, as a man of an unruly nature that knew he held her affection, yet had not the wherewithal to reward the men he attracted to his side. Such an image was dangerous, especially with a Queen on the throne, and with disarming frankness Bacon advised him to behave as a serious Councillor, spurning his easily-won popularity. But Essex would not listen to reason and went off to seek further glory in the expedition to the Azores, in which no prizes were taken. At Ferol he and Raleigh quarrelled violently, but Elizabeth's displeasure at the ill success of the voyage was mollified by Essex's safe return, and she cried for joy.

The Queen's happiness did not, however, mean that she would bow to her favourite's excessive demands for posts for

The English attack upon Cadiz in 1596. The
Spanish merchant ships are depicted huddled inside
the bay, defended by galleys, while the Dutch and
English ships appear in the foreground.

Francis Bacon, by an unknown artist. Francis was the youngest son of Nicholas Bacon (see p. 44). He received his training as a lawyer at the Inns of Court and by the 1590s he had become a protégé of Essex. Essex tried repeatedly, but unsuccessfully, to have Bacon appointed to office, but Elizabeth was wary of giving her favourite too much power. Ironically, Bacon served as one of the Queen's counsel at the trial of Essex after his rebellion. In the reign of James I he became Solicitor-General, Lord Keeper and Lord Chancellor.

his friends. Rather than have one of his nominees as Vice-Chamberlain she left the office vacant and Bacon, who had hoped for a remunerative legal post, was disappointed. Essex could get anything for himself, but nothing for his friends, complained one of them – though this view would have dismayed the Queen, who made great efforts to preserve a balance between the Essex and Cecil factions at court, even though she never put a man into an office he was incapable of filling. But Essex expected a monopoly of the Queen's patronage and had developed his own secretariat to deal with applications. He hurt Elizabeth by failing to attend her Accession Day festivities in 1597 and she was irritated by his absence from Parliament and Council. Bacon again warned him to 'dissemble like a courtier', taking Leicester as his example. Away from court the greatest favourite is never missed, forgetfulness breeds wrath 'and the wrath of a prince is as the roaring of a lion'. When at last Elizabeth promoted Lord Howard of Effingham to the earldom of Nottingham in 1597, Essex took exception to the wording of his patent, which praised Howard's service at Cadiz as well as in the Armada campaign. To keep the peace at court the Queen now appointed Essex Earl Marshal and he threw his weight about with marked disdain. When the appointment of a new Lord Lieutenant in Ireland was being discussed in Council everyone listened patiently to Essex's harangues, but when the Queen ruled against his nominee he turned his back on her in disgust. She cuffed him on the ear, telling him to leave the room, and foolishly he put his hand as if to draw his sword, but Nottingham stepped between him and the Queen. As he left he shouted that he would never have taken such an indignity sitting down, no, not even from Henry VIII, and went to sulk at his manor at Wanstead, writing a letter in high strain, for he could not bring himself to apologise to Elizabeth. Though she would dearly have had him back at court, any *rapprochement* must be on her terms: 'he hath played long enough upon me and now I mean to play awhile with him and stand as much upon my greatness as he hath upon his stomach.'

Old Burghley had prepared for his own succession by securing the appointment of his son Robert as Principal Secretary, while Essex was at sea, but he held on to the lord treasurership, as Winchester had done. When in his last illness in

1598, he offered to resign, Elizabeth would not hear of it, for she knew he wanted to die in harness. Years before, when Burghley had been melancholy and poorly with gout she had cheered him with a letter addressed to 'Sir Spirit', counselling him to 'be a good fellow'; now she came to his bedside at Burghley House to feed him with a spoon. Originally she had not cared for his brand of Protestantism, but he had mellowed wonderfully into an elder statesman, acquiring a detached political judgment second to none. No man had worked harder for her and though she could never forget that it was Burghley who had bullied her into signing Norfolk's death warrant and behaved in a less than straightforward way over the warrant for Mary, she knew these, like all his actions, had been animated by an unswerving sense of duty. He had proved the necessary counterpart to Leicester and now his son was already balancing the mercurial Essex.

Robert Cecil, his second son, was a politician to his fingertips and his development came as a relief to Burghley after the disappointments of his eldest son. Because Robert was a hunchback, men credited him with Machiavellian ways. His ability and industry were beyond question, but he lacked the inner religious zeal with which his father had been infected since his Cambridge days. Calculating, ambitious and quick to identify a political enemy, Robert made few friends and he enjoyed power not just for itself, but as a means to riches. The last decade of the reign was indeed characterised by a grasping attitude, and the cash nexus of public service that had always been present, yet decently subdued, now became blatant and insistent. The unsqueamish Robert Cecil made an appropriate chief minister for a materialistic age where his high-principled father would have been baffled and out of touch.

Ireland had remained an insoluble problem for Elizabeth, as for later sovereigns, and campaigns against a series of rebels cost her vast sums, while the fighting proved a graveyard of military reputations. The latest disaster, Tyrone's rout of an English army near Blackwater, brought Essex back to court offering his services as commander. The Queen still refused to see him, so he retired to Wanstead with a feigned illness that charmed her into forgiveness. She realised that only a forceful leader could hope for success against Tyrone and at last decided

Robert Cecil, 1st Earl of Salisbury, William Cecil's second son. He was a brilliant politician, hard-working and able. He made few friends and was distrusted and feared by many. He succeeded his father as Elizabeth's chief minister and largely engineered the accession of James I.

to take Essex at his own valuation; he left for Ireland in March 1599 with a considerable army, though Elizabeth had bound him by detailed instructions which, from the outset, he disobeyed. The Earl conferred knighthoods freely, encouraged his men to question the strategy of invading Ulster and instead of attacking Tyrone made a truce with him. Contrary to express orders forbidding his return, he left Ireland in a rage and by the morning of 28 September, through riding non-stop from Chester, he reached Nonsuch Palace. He strode upstairs to the private apartments, pushing aside everyone who tried to stop him, and burst into the sovereign's bedchamber. Elizabeth, only

just out of bed, had not begun her elaborate toilet, so Essex saw her as no man had ever seen her before; Gloriana without her wig and her rouge, her ruff and her mass of jewels, stripped, too, of the trappings of regality. Stunned by his arrival, she let him kiss her hand and then he left to change from his riding clothes, expecting to win his way with her by his charm which had never failed him. Later he explained to her his conduct of the Irish campaign, yet she absolutely refused to be taken in by his excuses and special pleading. After a grilling in Council he feared the Tower, but for the present found himself in the custody of the Lord Keeper at York House.

Elizabeth on her way to Nonsuch Palace in 1582, from an engraving by Hoefnagel. Nonsuch Palace was built by Henry VIII as his answer to Francis I's magnificent palace at Chambord. In the second half of her reign Elizabeth visited Nonsuch each summer to go hunting.

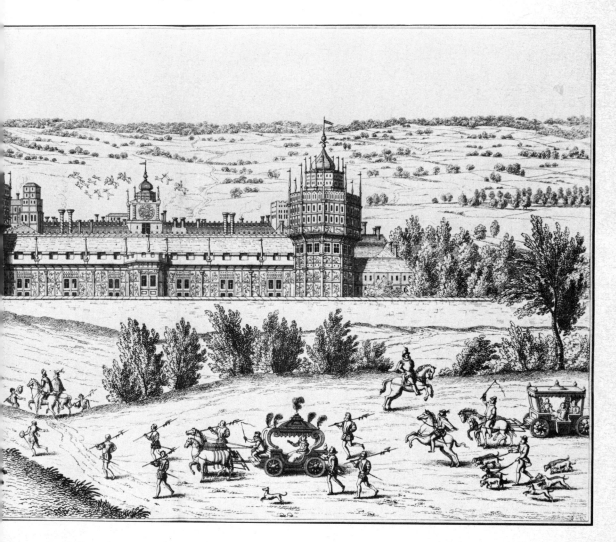

He became ill from fear and worry – so ill that the Queen sent her doctors to tend him and he was prayed for in London churches, to her great annoyance. Plans made for his trial were cancelled when he wrote a grovelling submission, detailing his faults, though Elizabeth still would not write to him. He was spared proceedings in the Star Chamber that many thought he deserved, but he had still to appear in June before the judges who censured him for his utter mismanagement of the Irish campaign, and he learnt that he was to be confined in his own house in the Strand at the Queen's pleasure, deprived of all his offices. Elizabeth made him wait another three months before setting him free, though since he was forbidden the court he still regarded himself as a prisoner, announcing that he would retire from public life.

Essex's chief worry now was not his reputation but his enormous debts, for the chief source of his income, the lease of the duties on sweet wines, expired at Michaelmas and if Elizabeth were not to renew it he would be finished. He pleaded on paper with her as her 'humblest, faithfullest and more than most devoted vassal', and as she read his messages she knew she had him beaten. The Earl of Essex had a lesson to learn that was long overdue; she would not renew his patent, but instead of granting the wine duties to someone else she would keep them in her own hands and if he showed he could behave himself there would be a chance of his receiving a fresh grant. His star had fallen and, megalomaniac that he had become, he could not accept the cruel fact.

The Queen's conditions for curbing him, he swore, were 'as crooked as her carcass'. Harington who paid a visit to Essex House was appalled by his state of mind, for with bankruptcy fast approaching he was being urged by the adventurers in his camp to try a last gamble: if charm would not make Elizabeth alter her mind, then force could. The chief plotters at Essex House included the Earl of Southampton and Lord Mountjoy's son, who like Essex both looked upon a *coup d'état* as the only way of solving their acute financial difficulties. Indeed there was not one man of note in their camp who was solvent – an indication of Cecil's success in depriving the Essex faction of court patronage. In addition, there were men who had served under the Earl in Ireland, France, or at sea, and had become so mesmerised by his powers of leadership that they thought it a crime that he was not the Queen's chief minister in place of the devious Cecil. As in 1569 conspiracy was the sole path that 'Her Majesty's opposition', under the Tudor constitution, could tread. Essex was prepared for a change of sovereign if a change of government could not be effected with Elizabeth on the throne. Essex's revolt was much more critical and dramatic than the Northern Rebellion of 1569, because it was staged in the capital, and its leader was reckoned by many the most popular man in all England. The conspirators paid the actors at *The Globe* to play *Richard II* as a declaration of intent that could not be misunderstood; if they could not rescue the Queen from evil advisers and engineer Essex's appointment as Lord Protector then they would not stop at killing her. To restrain Essex in his foolhardiness he was summoned to court, but dared not obey, so on Sunday, 8 February 1601 the Queen's men came to Essex House to reason with him; instead of persuading him to submit they were themselves made prisoners. His followers urged an attack on Whitehall, where Elizabeth was residing, but the Earl rode past Temple Bar intending to make the City his stronghold, shouting: 'For the Queen, For the Queen! A plot is laid for my life.' A herald followed in his wake proclaiming him a traitor and soon it was all over, for the City of London, which Elizabeth had courted before her accession, remained steadfast to her. Apprentices, who were wont to cheer the favourite and offer to die in his service, would not take up arms against their Queen. She told the French ambassador that night that 'a senseless ingrate had at last revealed what had long been in his mind'. Essex cleared any doubts about his intended treachery during his trial, boasting the Queen could not be safe so long as he lived.

She signed his death warrant on Shrove Tuesday but did not at once send it to the Lieutenant of the Tower, perhaps to give the condemned man the chance of begging for a reprieve. He knew he could expect no mercy from Elizabeth, or from those about her, and next day was executed. No more than thirty-four, he was the only person since Christopher Hatton's death that she had really cared for, but for him Elizabeth was no more than an old lady, to be exploited for her wealth and influence. Despite the Earl's great popularity, public opinion came down

'*A senseless ingrate had at last revealed what had long been in his mind*'

OVERLEAF The funeral cortège of Elizabeth I, from a contemporary painting by William Camden, Elizabeth's body was taken by water from Richmond to Whitehall, and her funeral took place on 28 April 1603 at Westminster. Her effigy, which can be seen on the coffin, was fully dressed and crowned. There were sixteen hundred mourners and the figures depicted around the coffin are the Gentlemen Pensioners.

The Chariott drawne by foure Horses vpon which Charret
stood the Coffin couered wth purple Veluett and vpon
that the reprefentation, The Canapy borne by six Knights.

footemen.

Gentlemen Pentioners   Gentlemen Pentioners

firmly on her side – rightly the Queen had taken the Knave, said the ballads. It was Robert Cecil, not his sovereign, who was given the blame for Essex's end:

> Little Cecil trips up and down
> He rides both Court and Crown

The Commons, summoned in 1601 to vote heavy taxes for the vigorous conduct of the continuing war against Spain and the campaign against the Irish rebels, at once turned to the grievance of monopolies, for the Queen had not kept her promise made in the last Parliament to reform the system, and soon government business was at a standstill. Monopolies granted to courtiers had increased the cost of living, for many of them concerned everyday commodities. With her touch as sure as ever, the Queen intervened, promising widespread reforms and even undertook to cancel various patents. The House was so delighted that members asked to send a deputation to thank her for her magnanimity, and when she agreed to receive a hundred members in the Council room at Whitehall, they said they all wanted to come. Here Mr Speaker on his knees told her they would willingly expend their 'last drops of blood' in serving her and she answered with an oration that was to be acclaimed as her 'golden speech', for in it she distilled the essence of that unique relationship between sovereign and subjects in the golden age of monarchy. Her greatest jewel was their love for her, her greatest achievement to be Queen over so thankful a people. Though she knew well enough that she would have to answer on judgment day for her rule on earth, 'there will never queen sit in my seat with more zeal to my country, care for my subjects and that sooner with willingness will venture her life for your good and safety than myself. And though you have had, and may have, many princes more mighty and wise, sitting in this state, yet you never had, or shall have any that will be more careful and loving'. She ended with thankfulness to God for his manifold mercies – not least in giving her a fearless heart.

Outwardly at least she had achieved a harmonious relationship with her faithful Commons. The long battles about the succession and marriage, and the campaigns of the Puritans in Parliament for a root and branch reform of the Church on presbyterian lines, which had persisted from 1559 to 1593, had been fought and won, for she had never given an inch, regularly vetoing their bills about the Church. Men like the Wentworth brothers, Peter and Paul, had endured imprisonment for linking religious reform with the right of Parliamentary free speech, for Elizabeth had seen their demands to range widely over affairs as an attack on her prerogative. She had never underrated the dangers of Puritanism or of the 'prophesying' movement within the established Church, and she warned James of Scotland 'there is risen both in your realm and mine a sect of perilous consequence, such as would have no kings but a presbytery'. The writings and sermons of Edmund Cartwright, a Cambridge professor with powerful friends at court and in the House of Commons, had given the Presbyterian movement an intellectual basis, while the series of Martin Marprelate's tracts mocked at the establishment. At last a considered reply to the troublesome Cartwright and his fellows had been made by the judicious Dr Richard Hooker, in his *Laws of Ecclesiastical Polity*, which showed the Queen to be on the side of the angels and her religious policy sanctified by reason. The Puritans in and out of Parliament bided their time in these last years of the reign hoping that a change of sovereign would produce a change in policy, while the Catholics, too, were hopeful though their ranks had been weakened by the archpriest controversy.

Three weeks after her 'golden speech' Elizabeth went to the Lords for the dissolution and made a masterly survey of domestic and foreign affairs, looking back to the Northern Rebellion and the defeat of the Armada and anticipating, now that Philip II was dead, an end to the war with Spain and the final overthrow of the rebels in Ireland. The most remarkable feature of her speech, which few who heard it realised was her swan song, was that she had not a word to say about the question that had remained unanswered ever since her accession, the name of her successor.

She wrote obscure letters to James VI, feeling he should have the wit to read between the lines: 'Let not shades deceive you, which may take away best substance from you, when they can turn but to dust or smoke.' It was as if he had dared to ask the unforgivable question and received an 'answer answerless'; yet she sent him her fond wishes and asked him to scan her words

'You have had ... many princes more mighty and wise ... yet you never had any ... more careful and loving'

The Essex Rebellion

This took place in February 1601. The chief plotters at Essex House were young noblemen who looked to a rebellion to solve their financial troubles. The rebellion was dramatic and short – it was also the last revolt against Elizabeth's authority.

BELOW The death-warrant of Essex, with Elizabeth's bold signature at the head.

LEFT Henry Wriothesley, 3rd Earl of Southampton, one of Essex's co-rebels. He commissioned this portrait to commemorate his years in the Tower after the rebellion.

RIGHT Thomas Lee by Marcus Gheeraerts. He was the nephew of Sir Henry Lee, Elizabeth's Champion at the Tilt. He sought his fortunes in Ireland and is depicted here as an Irish knight with bare legs to help him through the watery bogs. Thomas took part in the Essex rebellion and was executed at Tyburn.

'as becometh a king'. As he patiently deciphered the untidy regal scrawl that in the old days would have made Ascham, her writing-master, weep, James Stuart rejoiced that the throne of England was still to be his. As shrewd as ever, Elizabeth knew that people very near her were cautiously making plans, with Robert Cecil looking over his shoulder towards the rising sun, just as his father had done in Mary's reign; while more than one of the maids-of-honour was postponing marriage, gambling that Elizabeth would not be alive to obstruct and reprove. It was a court now of whispers and coded messages. Elizabeth told Lambarde, the antiquary, 'now the wit of the fox is everywhere on foot, so hardly one faithful or virtuous man may be found'. She could afford to regard the scene with a wry humour, for what happened a few months hence would be their affair and she would have no part to play.

The execution of Essex had ended any effective opposition to Robert Cecil, yet the Secretary's authority was very far from being absolute, since it was limited by the Queen herself and would not necessarily last beyond her life. Cecil had felt bound to enter into negotiations with James VI without compromising his position with the Queen. 'The Queen indeed is my sovereign', he wrote, 'and I am her creature. I may not least deceive her.' Having a cautious eye on the future was rather different from planning a present *coup*, as Essex had so disastrously attempted. Sir Robert wrote secretly to James advising him on the safest means of proceeding on the demise of the Crown so there would be no hiatus, for that would surely cast him into limbo and the kingdom into a turmoil. Once the moment arrived he would issue the accession proclamation on his own responsibility and produce his own Greek chorus to shout loyally, as the kingmaker's messenger rode north. James's peaceful accession at Whitehall would ensure the continuing power of Cecil at the centre of affairs, despite the influx of Scottish favourites. But all this was for the future.

The forty-fourth anniversary of Elizabeth's accession was greeted with incredible applause, almost as if people predicted she would never see another 17 November. Sir John Harington was much struck by her increasing frailty and melancholy, even if to the less observant she seemed little altered, putting on a

brave face to enjoy the round of Christmas plays and the dancing in the Privy Chamber. Harington wrote to his wife: 'My royal godmother, and this state's natural mother, doth now bear show of human infirmity too fast for that evil we shall get by her death and too slow for that good which we shall get by her releasement from her pains and misery.' She had asked him to see her – a blessed moment for him, until he saw how weak she was, with no appetite for food or, indeed, for life itself. She asked him about his writing and he showed her some verses, but she shook her head; when he felt Time

213

John Whitgift, Elizabeth's last Archbishop of Canterbury, whom she nicknamed her 'little black husband'. He was at Elizabeth's deathbed.

knocking at the gate, as she did, foolish versifying would have no pleasure, for 'I am past my relish for such matters'. In mid-January she left Whitehall, which the astrologer John Dee had warned her to avoid, for Richmond Palace, as a 'warm winter box to shelter her old age' and here a month later she was taken ill. Hunsdon's son, Robert Carey, came to cheer her in those weary days and worse nights, when she could not bear the thought of going to bed, but snatched at sleep from her chair or cushions on the floor, distressing her ladies, complaining of a fiendish dryness in her mouth and the miseries of insomnia.

214

'No Robin, I *am not well*', she told Carey with many sighs. Howard the Lord Admiral tried his best with her, but she answered, 'My Lord, I am tied with a chain of iron about my neck'. He told her she had never lacked courage, but she would not have it; 'I am tied, I am tied and the case is altered with me.'

Those last days naturally gave rise to many legends, not least about the succession. It would have been quite uncharacteristic of Elizabeth to have indicated James as her successor to her Councillors round her bed at Richmond; she could not at the end have named him, for by then she had lost all power of speech. On the journey from Whitehall to Richmond ten weeks earlier she was reputed to have said to Howard: 'I told you my seat has been the seat of kings, and I will have no rascal to succeed me; and who should succeed me but a king?' By itself this has the hallmark of truth, but it would have been impossible for her to have continued, as the narrative of their conversation has it, by asking a further question, 'Who but our cousin of Scotland?' She had deliberately refused to name her successor for forty-four years and she was too determined a character, even though under the shadow of death, to make a mockery now of one of her few consistencies by breaking her silence.

To scotch rumours that might prejudice public order the Council had forbidden news about the Queen's health to be published. At morning service on 23 March, as the bishops prayed for her recovery, there were tears in many eyes and throughout that day Archbishop Whitgift waited to be summoned to her side. Her 'little black husband', as she had called him, had been favoured because, unlike Matthew Parker, he had stayed celibate and, unlike Edmund Grindal, he had taken a sensible attitude towards doctrine and Church discipline, which she had applauded. At 6 p.m. he was called in to his Queen and Supreme Governor. By signs she affirmed her sure belief in the Holy Trinity and the mercifulness of the Almighty. Holding her hand as he knelt by the great bed, he kept a long vigil in prayer until she had fallen asleep, at last at peace with the world. She died in her sleep about 3 a.m. on 24 March, the last day of the year by the old computation. Before the state funeral, the son of Mary Stuart had already begun his progress south and was only waiting for the obsequies to end before taking possession of Whitehall.

Elizabeth's body was brought by water from Richmond to Whitehall for her funeral in Westminster Abbey at the end of April, and in procession the customary effigy on the coffin seemed so lifelike, fully dressed and bearing the regalia, that it provoked 'a general sighing, groaning and weeping' among Londoners. There was no precedent in the whole of history, thought the chronicler Stow, for this universal grief, 'for any people, time or state to make like lamentations for the death of their sovereign'. Elizabeth Tudor was the first English monarch to give her name to an age, and this in spite of being a woman.

James VI of Scotland, who became James I of England, on Elizabeth's death on 24 March 1603.

Select bibliography

THE QUEEN

Since Mandell Creighton's *Queen Elizabeth* in 1896 (reissued 1966*
with an introduction by G.R.Elton) there have been full-scale
biographies of Elizabeth I by Sir John Neale (1934*), by Elizabeth
Jenkins (1958*) and by Neville Williams (1967*), and a shorter study
by Joel Hurstfield, *Elizabeth I and the Unity of England* (1960*).

G.B.Harrison has edited *The Letters of Queen Elizabeth* (1935,
revised 1968), while Roy Strong has made a study of *The Portraits of
Queen Elizabeth I* (1963).

THE REIGN

The most detailed narrative is J.A.Froude's *History of England from
the Fall of Wolsey to the Defeat of the Spanish Armada* (1856–70) volumes
VII-XII, also available in 'Everyman's Library'. An American
historian, E.P.Cheyney, continued this narrative on a similar scale
in *A History of England from the Defeat of the Armada to the Death of
Elizabeth* (2 vols, 1914, 1918).

Shorter accounts of the reign will be found in J.B.Black *The Reign
of Elizabeth, 1558–1603* (Oxford History of England vol. viii, 1936;
2nd edition revised 1959); S.T.Bindoff, *Tudor England* (1950*);
G.R.Elton, *England Under the Tudors* (1956*) and A.F.Pollard,
Political History of England, 1547–1603 (1910).

R.B.Wernham surveys England's foreign relations in *Before the
Armada; the Growth of English Foreign Policy*. Lacy Baldwin Smith,
The Elizabethan Epic (1966*) places the achievements of the reign in a
European context, while Garrett Mattingly devotes a whole book to
The Defeat of the Spanish Armada (1959*).

SOCIETY

A.L.Rowse, *The England of Elizabeth* (1950*) and *The Expansion of
Elizabethan England* (1953*); Wallace MacCaffrey, *The Shaping of the
Elizabethan Regime* (1969); J.E.Neale, *Essays in Elizabethan History*
(1958*) and *The Elizabethan House of Commons* (1949*); Christopher
Hill, *Society and Puritanism* (1956); Joel Hurstfield, *The Queen's Wards*

*Titles marked with an asterisk are also available in a paperback edition.

(1958); Lawrence Stone, *The Crisis of the Aristocracy* (1965*); Muriel St Claire Byrne, *Elizabethan Life in Town and Country* (1925; revised 1961*) and A. V. Judges *The Elizabethan Underworld* (reprints of tracts and ballads, 1930).

LIVES

Among the many biographies of contemporary figures and countries the most readable are: Antonia Fraser, *Mary Queen of Scots* (1969*); Edith Sitwell, *The Queens and the Hive* (1962*), an account of the clash of personalities between the English and Scottish Queens; Conyers Read, *Mr Secretary Cecil and Queen Elizabeth* (1955*) and *Lord Burghley and Queen Elizabeth* (1960*); Elizabeth Jenkins, *Elizabeth and Leicester* (1961); E. St John Brooks, *Sir Christopher Hatton* (1946); A. L. Rowse, *Raleigh and the Throckmortons* (1962); William M. Wallace, *Sir Walter Raleigh* (1959); Robert Lacey, *Robert, Earl of Essex* (1971) and P. M. Handover, *The Second Cecil, 1563–1604*, a life of Robert, later first Earl of Salisbury (1959).

MISCELLANEOUS

E. K. Chambers, *The Elizabethan Stage* (4 vols. 1923); Julian S. Corbet, *Drake and the Tudor Navy* (2 vols 1898–9); C. G. Cruikshank, *Elizabeth's Army* (1946); E. H. Fellows, *The English Madrigal Composers* (1921); Erna Auerbach, *Tudor Artists* (1954); and G. D. Ramsay, *English Overseas Trade during the Centuries of Emergence* (1957).

Most of the above have full bibliographies.

Acknowledgments

Photographs and illustrations were supplied by, or are reproduced by kind permission of the following. The photographs on pages 10-11, *14*, 42/1, 68 are reproduced by gracious permission of H.M. the Queen; on page 34 by gracious permission of the Duke of Bedford; on page 53 by courtesy of the Archbishop of Canterbury (copyright reserved by the Courtauld Institute of Art and the Church Commissioners); on pages *82-3* by courtesy of the Marquess of Salisbury, K.G.; on page 124 (*above*) by courtesy of the Marquess of Bath: on page 140 by courtesy of Lord Petre; on page 162 by kind permission of the Duke of Atholl; on page 173 by kind permission of Lord De L'Isle, Penhurst Place; on page 210 (*above*) by gracious permission of the Duke of Buccleuch and Queensbury; and on page 210 (*below*) by courtesy of His Grace the Duke of Sutherland. Ashmolean Museum, Oxford: 16, 46-7/1, 143; Bodleian Library, Oxford: 47, 103, 161; BPC: 130-1, 151, 159, *173*, 182; British Museum: 21, 38-39, 46-7/2, 78-9, 113, 128-9, 130-1, 141/1, 141/2, 151, 156-7, 159, 171, 182-3, 184-5, *194/1*, *194/2*, *206-7*; Courtauld Institute: 147; Dulwich College Picture Gallery: 152/1; Kerry Dundas: 104, 104-5, 106-7; Essex Record Office: 140; Mary Evans Picture Library: 71, 149, 158; Werner Forman: 190-1; John Freeman: 78-9, *82-3*, 179; Ian Graham: *15*; Hardwick Hall (National Trust): 106/1; André Held, Lausanne: 118-9; H.M. Stationery Office: 84-5; A.F.Kersting: 17; Lambeth Palace: 53; Mansell Collection: 99, 108, 116, 134-5, 152/2, 153/2, 153/3, *176*, 188, *194/1*, *194/2*, 203; Musée Cantonal des Beaux-Arts, Lausanne, 118-9; National Galleries of Scotland: *176*, 210/1; National Maritime Museum: 187, 199; National Monuments Record: 100-1, 107; National Portrait Gallery, London: 2, 13, 20, 22, 23, 29, 42/2, 43/1, 43/2, 43/3, 54, 89, 114, 124/2, 125, 148, 153/1, 160, *164/1*, 167, 178, 183, *195*, 200, 214, 216; Nottingham Castle Museum: 213; Public Record Office, London: 30, 31, 65, 182, 189; Radio Times Hulton Picture Library: 24-5, 74; Tom Scott: 162; Sydney Sussex College, Cambridge: 59; Sir John Soane's Museum: 147; Tate Gallery London (on loan from Captain Loel Guiness): 211; Victoria and Albert Museum, London: 3, 62-3, 66-7, 75/1, 75/2, 109, 112/1, 112/2, 112/3, 138, 142, 144, 144-5, *164/2*; Walker Art Gallery, Liverpool: 12; Warwick Castle Collection: 48; Dean and Chapter of Westminster: 190-1; Simon Wingfield-Digby Esq: *94-5*.

Genealogical trees

HOUSE OF TUDOR

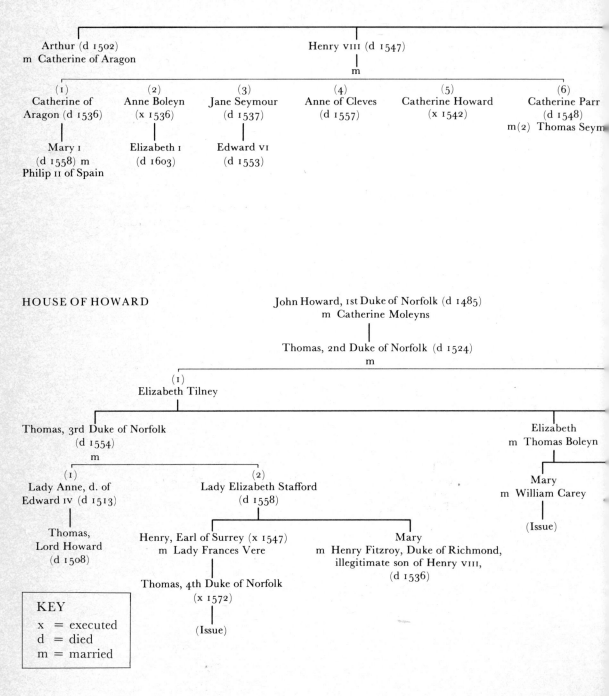

Arthur (d 1502)
m Catherine of Aragon

Henry VIII (d 1547)
m

(1) Catherine of Aragon (d 1536)
(2) Anne Boleyn (x 1536)
(3) Jane Seymour (d 1537)
(4) Anne of Cleves (d 1557)
(5) Catherine Howard (x 1542)
(6) Catherine Parr (d 1548) m(2) Thomas Seym

Mary I (d 1558) m Philip II of Spain
Elizabeth I (d 1603)
Edward VI (d 1553)

HOUSE OF HOWARD

John Howard, 1st Duke of Norfolk (d 1485)
m Catherine Moleyns

Thomas, 2nd Duke of Norfolk (d 1524)
m

(1) Elizabeth Tilney

Thomas, 3rd Duke of Norfolk (d 1554)
m

Elizabeth
m Thomas Boleyn

(1) Lady Anne, d. of Edward IV (d 1513)
(2) Lady Elizabeth Stafford (d 1558)

Mary
m William Carey

Thomas, Lord Howard (d 1508)

Henry, Earl of Surrey (x 1547)
m Lady Frances Vere

Mary
m Henry Fitzroy, Duke of Richmond, illegitimate son of Henry VIII, (d 1536)

(Issue)

Thomas, 4th Duke of Norfolk (x 1572)

(Issue)

KEY
x = executed
d = died
m = married

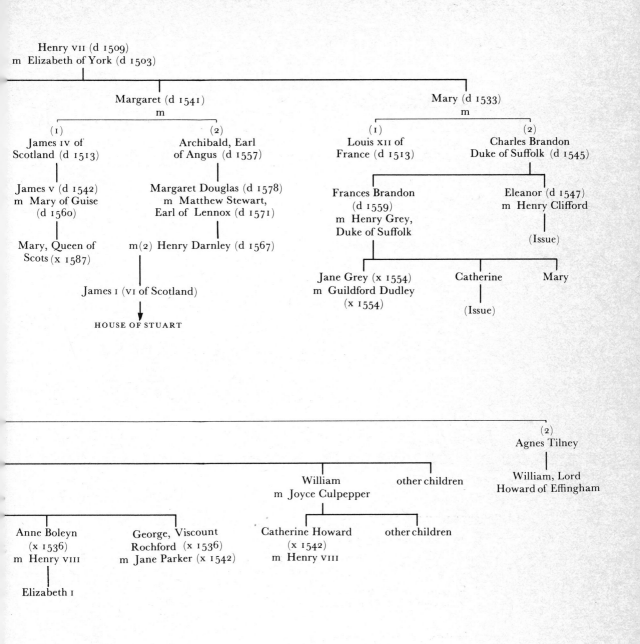

Henry VII (d 1509)
m Elizabeth of York (d 1503)

Margaret (d 1541)
m

(1)
James IV of
Scotland (d 1513)

(2)
Archibald, Earl
of Angus (d 1557)

James V (d 1542)
m Mary of Guise
(d 1560)

Margaret Douglas (d 1578)
m Matthew Stewart,
Earl of Lennox (d 1571)

Mary, Queen of
Scots (x 1587)

m(2) Henry Darnley (d 1567)

James I (VI of Scotland)

HOUSE OF STUART

Mary (d 1533)
m

(1)
Louis XII of
France (d 1513)

(2)
Charles Brandon
Duke of Suffolk (d 1545)

Frances Brandon
(d 1559)
m Henry Grey,
Duke of Suffolk

Eleanor (d 1547)
m Henry Clifford

(Issue)

Jane Grey (x 1554)
m Guildford Dudley
(x 1554)

Catherine

Mary

(Issue)

(2)
Agnes Tilney

William, Lord
Howard of Effingham

William
m Joyce Culpepper

other children

Anne Boleyn
(x 1536)
m Henry VIII

George, Viscount
Rochford (x 1536)
m Jane Parker (x 1542)

Catherine Howard
(x 1542)
m Henry VIII

other children

Elizabeth I

Index

(Note: *Peers and bishops are entered here under either the family name or the title, whichever makes for easier identification. For instance the Earl of Arundel appears under 'Arundel' (not as 'Fitzalan') while Lord Burghley appears as 'Cecil, William'; Archbishop Parker is entered under 'Parker', but John Leslie is placed under 'Ross, Bishop of'. Cross-references have been kept to a minimum.*)

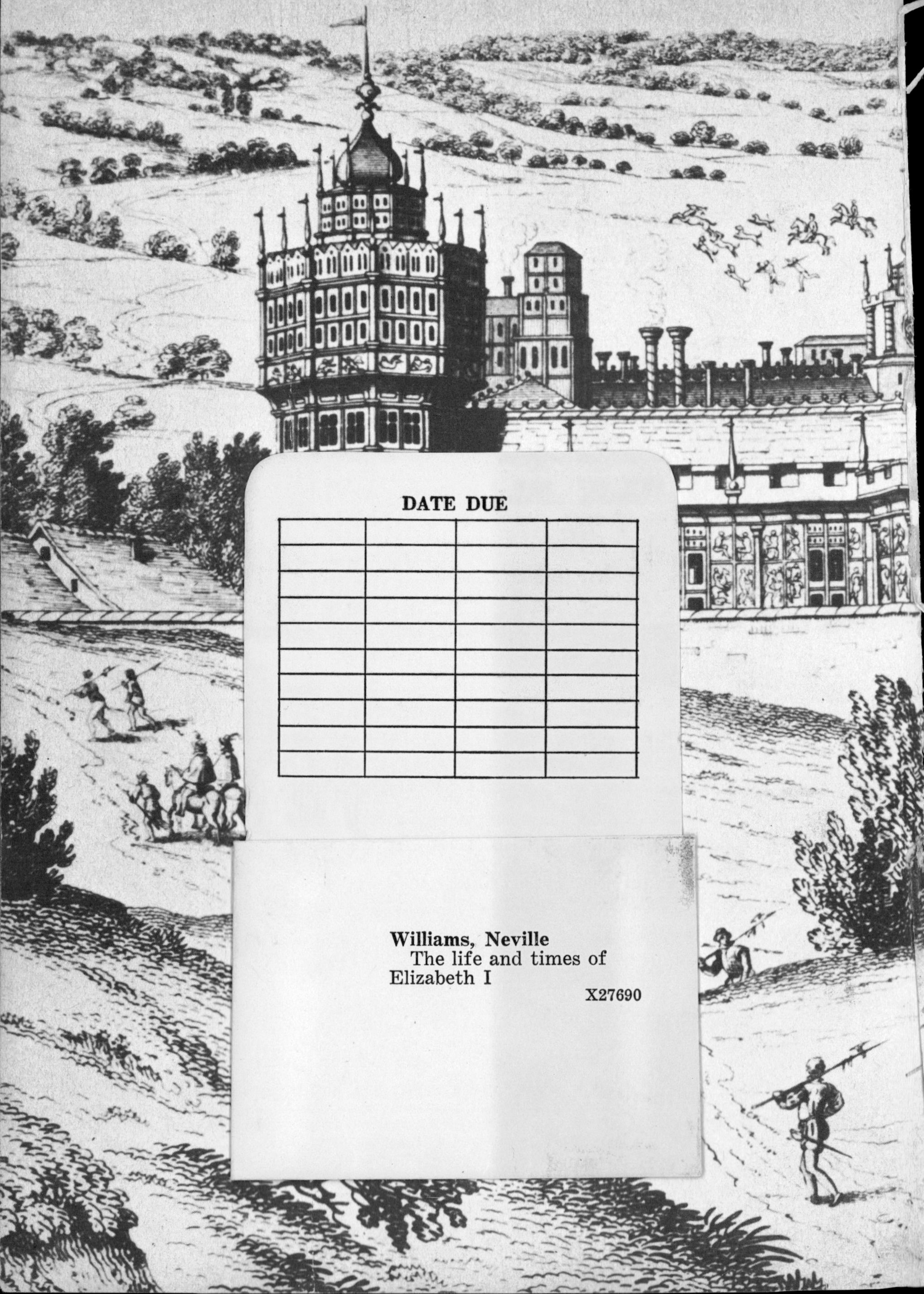